No More Peanut Butter Sandwiches

A father, a son with special needs, and their journey with God

Jeff Davidson

THANKS FOR ALL YOU
DO SU! GRATEFUL
FOR YOUR HEART FOR
SPECIAL NEEDS !

CROSSLINK
PUBLISHING

LUKE 14: 12 · 14

No More Peanut Butter Sandwiches: A father, a son with special needs, and their journey with God

P̶C̶ CrossLink Publishing
www.crosslinkpublishing.com

ISBN 978-1-63357-001-6

Library of Congress Control Number: 2014942589

For Becky and Jon Alex

I'm an ordinary man who married Wonder Woman and is raising Superman. I am so thankful that God chose to put us together as a family. I am a better father, a better husband, a better man, and a better follower of Christ because you two are in my life.

ACKNOWLEDGEMENTS AND THANKS

To Becky ... God's choices are perfect. I'm so glad he chose you to be my wife and Jon Alex's mother. There is no one in this world I love and respect more than you. Thank you for being my Wonder Woman.

To Jon Alex ... God's choices are indeed perfect. I'm so glad he chose you to be my son and for me to be your dad. I always thought I would be the teacher and you would be the student. How backwards I had it.

To the team at Rising Above Ministries, including April Phillips, Chris Pierce, and our amazing ministry leaders, volunteers, and supporters ... I love doing ministry with such a dedicated, gifted, and talented team. You're our family and I'm glad God chose to put you in our lives.

To our families, the Davidsons and Mitchells ... thank you for believing in the dream and the way you love and support our family.

To the man who prefers to remain nameless...your support of our ministry and belief in the vision are helping change the world for special-needs families.

To Barb Dittrich at comfortinthemidstofchaos.com … the first special-needs blogger who took a chance on an unknown writer, let him begin blogging on her site, and encouraged him that he had what it takes to write.

To the special-needs families we've met through Rising Above… you all have a story to tell. It's an honor and privilege to know you. You have my deepest respect and admiration. Thank you for allowing me to serve you.

To Rick Bates and the team at Crosslink Publishing … when everyone told me a first-time author couldn't get a publisher, you believed I had a story worth telling and a message worth sharing.

To all the special-needs families who just quietly go about life without fanfare … you may not get much admiration or encouragement on earth, but in heaven they are giving you a standing ovation.

TABLE OF CONTENTS

PREFACE

I have been a dad of a son with special needs for almost seventeen years now.

No one can possibly prepare you for the challenges of raising a child with special needs.

When you first begin the journey as a parent of a child with special needs, well-meaning friends and family will say things to try to encourage or comfort you. Unless someone has personally traveled down this path, though, one cannot truly grasp the effect it has on every aspect of life.

A special-needs family can have its entire world turned upside down. No part of life is left unscathed by the challenges. Initially, and at points along the way, it's very difficult to believe that God has a plan and a purpose for the experience. It's even harder at first for some to grasp that God has given you the most amazing and incredible gift through this child with special needs.

I believe God chose me to be the dad of a child with profound special needs. God also called me to become a special-needs missionary. I started and lead a national special-needs ministry birthed from my own experiences as a parent of a son with autism, cerebral palsy, and a seizure disorder.

Special-needs families are my people. I live, work, and do life together with people in the special-needs community.

I wrote this book because my people are dying. Emotionally, relationally, mentally, and spiritually—my people are dying.

I wrote this book to share my own experiences and try to give life to all those who are walking down this journey raising children with special needs.

This book is for all of you struggling with your challenges and the journey you have been placed on by God. Raising a child with special needs can seem like such a burden to many people. I want to show you just how truly blessed you really are and help you understand the gift you have been given.

Through this journey, you will experience pain, grief, and challenges. However, God is going to reveal himself to you in ways you have never dreamed or imagined.

If I can write anything here to encourage you, inspire you, or give you hope, then I am honored. You definitely inspire me with the way you persevere, endure, and continue to love your children unconditionally.

All of heaven stands and applauds for you, because every child is wonderfully made, created for a plan and a purpose, and destined to glorify God.

This book is also for anyone going through a trial, a situation, or a challenge, and struggling to find God's purpose in the pain.

Chapter 1
WHAT YOU DO WITH IT IS UP TO YOU

I sat on the worn dirt patch beside the weeping willow tree and tried to focus my eyes through the tears.

I felt everything and yet I felt nothing, all at the same time. My thoughts were on fire but my heart was stone-cold.

I felt like I had been betrayed, deceived, and outright misled. And, worst of all, I felt like the person who did it to me didn't even care.

I really began to wonder if he had ever existed in the first place. He was God. But I wasn't sure he was my God anymore.

For months and months, Becky and I had prayed and petitioned God for a healthy baby. Every night we lifted our petitions to God. We stormed heaven's throne room. We recited scriptures over and over. We claimed God's promises, and we stood on his Word. We praised God and we pledged our lives to him forever.

All we wanted was a healthy little baby to call our own.

Now a few months later, for the eighteenth night in a row, I had walked down the street from our little house.

I had stuck the stork sign from Baptist Hospital into the front yard of that house when we brought our son home. I had decorated a room in that house just for him, a room that held the baby bed, the toys, and the roomful of prayers that I had offered up for him long before he was ever born.

That house was now the reminder of dreams that had died and promises that were broken.

God had chosen not to give me a healthy, typical, little boy. Instead, God had chosen me to be the dad of child with special needs. God had given me a boy with autism and cerebral palsy. God had given me a little boy with such profound special needs he wouldn't be able to talk or even walk on his own. A little boy who would require our 24/7 care all of his life—from eating, bathing, getting dressed, moving around—all the basic functions of life.

Every night, a little bit more of me died as we came to terms with our new reality. I was living on the outside and dying on the inside.

So night after night, I walked down the street to the little weeping willow tree by the brook, and I sat on the dirt patch. Night after night I just cried.

I would scream at God, shake my fist at God, and pour out my hostility and my anger at him. I would cry, "Why did you do this to us?" I would yell, "Why do you hate us, what did we do to deserve this?"

I would remind him of all the prayers. I would remind him that we had been faithful to him, so why had he failed us?

I didn't just hurt. I ached to the core of my soul.

I needed an outlet and I decided that God would be my outlet. So I poured out my rage, my bewilderment, my frustration and my confusion on him.

Night after night I did that. Night after night I carried on this one-way conversation.

Night after night, God never said anything. Not a word.

I wasn't sure who was more dead, him or me.

Then, one night, I tried to cut God a deal. *Yea, that's the answer. I'm going to cut him a deal,* I thought. Really more like a bribe, but I figured it was worth trying.

That night, I told God that if he would only heal my son, then I would do everything I could to spread the word about how great God was. I would testify to his greatness, his miraculous provision, and to his healing.

I told God that if he would only heal my son, I would dedicate my life to serving him and testifying about our story for the rest of my life. I begged, I pleaded, and I negotiated.

I heard and felt nothing. All I got was a deafening silence.

Then one night as I sat weeping and sobbing, God broke his silence and spoke directly to my spirit and said, "I have given you a blessing, what you do with it is up to you."

I had no idea what that meant. I was in no shape to try to process it or make sense of it. How could this be a blessing? Was that even possible? This was a lifelong burden. How could anything good come of this?

What did God mean by saying, "I've given you a blessing, what you do with it is up to you?"

Chapter 2
THE UPSIDE-DOWN WORLD

When you first learn that your child has special needs or you receive a diagnosis, your entire world is rocked and turned upside down. Every aspect of your life is affected; nothing is left unscathed. From your morning routine, the way you go to work or school, the way you go shopping, go to church, or just simply run errands—everything changes.

Afternoon play dates are replaced with doctors and therapy appointments. Conversations with your spouse are dominated by discussion of treatment options, therapies, and your child's development.

At first, I began to dread going to other children's parties because I saw the other kids doing things my son could not do. I got depressed and discouraged so easily. So we stopped going to social events. Our friends saw our hurt and frustration but they didn't really know how to help. So, thinking it would help us, they stopped inviting us. But that just made the pain worse, because we began to feel even more alone and more different.

Every encounter with other children just led to comparison and added to the pain and the feeling that we were all alone. I begin keeping score of all the things the other kids my son's age could do that my son could not.

Secretly, I fantasized about building a massive bonfire out of those baby milestone books and having a giant book-burning party. I could see myself silhouetted against the shadows of this massive fire and I would invite all parents of children with special needs to come throw their milestone books on the fire as it stretched towards a blood-red sky. We would feel the glow of the fire against our faces as we shook our fists and raged at an unseen God.

As this new reality set in, several things began to happen. Gradually, a feeling of being overwhelmed and constantly dazed took over and left me in a very dark place.

I continually searched my heart and actions. "Had I done something to make God mad or want to punish me? Why had God turned his back on us and allowed this to happen? Who was at fault here, someone must be to blame?"

"Where was God?" Had he just left us here to figure this out on our own and just doesn't care anymore?

How could this have happened? Was God punishing us? Had we done something to cause his wrath? Who or what was at fault or to blame for this happening in our lives?

And if God is in control, why did he allow this to happen to us? We had prayed and prayed over this child while he was still in the womb. Where was this God I had banked on all my life?

Was God mad at just one of us or was he mad at both of us?

We had named our son Jonathan Alexander Davidson but we called him Jon Alex. We called him Jon Alex because every Southern boy should have two first names! Jonathan means, "gift from God" and Alexander means "conqueror."

Besides, his full name sounded so regal and majestic with a title like Senator or General in front of it. Now as we learned of his special needs, those names seemed like a cruel ironic joke.

I went about my days in a constant fog. The fog never lifted or lightened. And even worse, it never let go. The thoughts raced through my mind at all times of day and I lost total focus on my work and everything else. The negativity became relentless.

My wife Becky began to immediately research treatments, surfing online for therapy suggestions, supplements, and dietary options. She mobilized like she was going to battle. She declared war on what had happened and was determined to try to help our son as much as possible. She was constantly on the Internet or the phone with her handy notebooks always by her side.

But I'm a dad and, like most dads, I'm a fixer. Give me time to think and I really thought I could figure out the answer or solution to any problem. I could fix anything on my own. Stumped? Bring your problem to me and I will tell you how to fix it.

All of a sudden, I had this little boy with special needs and I was powerless to fix him. *I couldn't fix him.* Coming to that realization was an excruciating and wretched process. I had never before encountered anything in life I couldn't fix or overcome.

I am a self-admitted control freak and this was out of my hands. And I despised God and everyone else for it.

My coping mechanism, like so many other dads of children with special needs, was to live in denial. I convinced myself that this was temporary and he would eventually catch up developmentally. For years, I would not even utter the word "autism" out loud. I would say my son was on the autism spectrum, but not autistic. I would declare he had sensory processing issues but it wasn't autism. I acted as if as long as I didn't acknowledge it verbally, it didn't exist. I was convinced he would just grow out of it someday.

I would retreat at night to my home office and pour myself into my work, sitting at my desk until everyone else in the house was in bed. That's what most of us do when we are in denial or just don't know what to do. We retreat to something we are good at, or can master, and we throw ourselves into that instead. That's our coping mechanism.

So I dug in passionately at work and masked what was going on in my private life.

Coming to grips with the realization that you have a child with special needs is very much like many other life-altering significant moments in life. Everyone has to grieve. Everyone has to go through the grief process.

What no one tells you is that you and your spouse will grieve differently and not be at the same stage or place in your grief at the same time. Men, for example, tend to get all tangled up in the denial and anger stages of grief. We can linger there for years and, for many dads, it's unrecoverable. They never come to terms with it and it destroys them.

Some dads choose to live forever in anger or denial. Often, dads check out within just a few years of receiving a diagnosis. Many will just walk away and leave the family fatherless.

For too many others, though, they just become what I call the "vacant dad." The vacant dad stays in the marriage, but he is pretty much there in body only. He doesn't care, he doesn't get engaged, and he doesn't get involved. He's checked out in every way except physically. I don't know which is worse, the dad who leaves or the vacant dad. But I didn't want to be either one.

We have an epidemic of vacant dads in the special-needs community these days. We are losing too many dads within two or three years after diagnosis. As a result, single female caregivers are raising a generation of children with special needs by themselves.

Moms can sometimes struggle initially with blame or guilt. They blame their circumstances on themselves, something from the past, or something they did or didn't do. And they really struggle blaming God, and searching for answers.

This was a real battle for us as well. We live in a culture that tells us there is always someone to blame for everything. We began to live in fear that maybe we had caused this ourselves. Deep inside, many parents of children with special needs begin to blame themselves, and that just leads to further depression and despair. The questions and self-doubt never end and the answers never come.

We crave answers, though. That's really what new special-needs parents want. We want answers to questions. But what we don't realize is that we are asking the wrong questions.

What no one tells families like ours is that you don't go through the grief stages just once. Pop psychologists will tell you once you go through the grief stages and come to acceptance, you will be just fine.

That's a great relief. But there is one problem with that concept. It's a lie.

Grief returns all throughout this process. Every time your child enters a new stage in life or another traditional milestone is missed, you might go back through the grief process again and again. Different things trigger the grief cycle at different times for each member of the family.

The grief never really ends completely. With each new challenge, the grief cycle can be triggered all over again. If you don't learn how to manage the grief cycle and understand its stages, you can fall into chronic sorrow.

Living with chronic sorrow means never fully escaping the sadness and despair that is associated with having a child with special needs. You may have moments of respite, moments of acceptance, and fleeting moments of happiness—but the underlying chronic sorrow always lurks just below the surface of your heart.

I think most special-needs families live with the chronic sorrow. It just becomes part of the fabric of their lives. It's like a computer application that is always running in the background. I was that way myself initially.

But that was when I still thought my life's story was about me.

So we put on our plastic faces and appeared to the world as if everything was just fine in our world. We laughed on the outside while we were dying on the inside. We smiled all day and cried all night.

I would lay awake in the dark, exhausted but sleepless. I was acting as if I had it all together, but inside it was all falling apart.

When you first begin this walk, you feel as if you are walking down this path totally alone. You feel like no one, not even your family and close friends, can possibly understand your life.

Our family and friends didn't know how to relate or understand our new world. It wasn't that they didn't care, they just didn't understand how affected our lives were now. Some friends begin to drift away, and our family struggled with our new reality. We began to lose some friends, and the overwhelming feeling that we were all alone enveloped us.

I couldn't really process what had happened and how it affected our life. How was I supposed to be able to explain it to them?

Like many other special-needs families, our extended family struggled to grasp our new upside-down world. In many ways, they had an unrealistic notion that our life hadn't been affected very much. Their expectations for normal family life were often so out of line with the new reality.

No one knows how exactly to act around you or your child. They are a little unsure what to even say. Family get-togethers and holidays can become so stressful, awkward, and even painful from the elephant in the room.

The same thing happens with your friends. There is a nervous awkwardness at first when they are around you. This just complicates your own feelings that no one close to you knows or understands what you are going through in this new upside-down world.

By the time I had graduated college, I thought I had my whole life planned out. I knew exactly what I wanted to accomplish by certain times and dates in my life, and I was extremely goal-oriented.

I had certain career goals and I was not prepared to have to sacrifice those dreams or lay down those goals. I never had planned or expected to be a dad of a child with special needs. Who does?

Now, my new normal required that I lay down some of those dreams and goals for the future. That's a hard hurdle for a lot of dads. In our pride and self-assurance, we think we can still make it all work without sacrifice.

A lot of dads of children with special needs are never able to accept that point. They refuse to believe that they have to make sacrifices of their own, or they simply are not prepared to do so.

Stubbornly not willing to yield, dads will live in denial, anger, and bitterness for years. Oftentimes, those emotions are transferred to other family members just escalating tensions, and often exploding like hidden landmines.

For those who do accept the need to change their plans in order to walk through this journey, they can still battle resentment, bitterness, and silent despair over the fact that they have to lay down certain dreams and plans for life.

Initially, we made the same near-fatal mistake that so many special-needs families make as well.

The biggest enemy of any newly diagnosed family is isolation. And it's the biggest mistake a special-needs parent will ever make.

We began to withdraw socially and isolate ourselves. We began to do what so many other families of children with autism do. We withdrew in to the cave of autism with its cold hard floors, its windowless walls, and its deep caverns of loneliness and bitterness.

Isolation will kill you mentally, emotionally, and spiritually. Families begin to stay home as much as possible. They close the blinds to their hearts and emotions and won't let anyone peek inside.

Autism became my bunker. I retreated to my bunker and hid out from the world. You don't think anyone can possibly understand what you are experiencing. Add that to the fact that you think no one else is going through what you are experiencing, and it's a toxic combination.

I would go to work and everyone would share about their child's latest experiences and accomplishments. I would hear about the sports they were playing, the hobbies they were pursuing, and their school activities or career aspirations.

I would remain silent about my own son. I didn't talk about my kid with special needs much because I didn't feel anyone else could relate or understand. And so we kept stacking bricks up on our wall of isolation we were building. Some men will work side by side for years next to another man and never mention having a child with special needs.

Knowing that your child isn't going to have those same experiences or ever achieve those accomplishments becomes a daily reminder of just how different your life has become.

You beg doctors and therapists to tell you this is only temporary. You plead for a promise that substantial, if not miraculous, progress can be made. You cling to even the faintest glimmer of hope that the situation will change. But no one can give you that answer.

I remember still insisting my son was just developmentally delayed even when he was seven years old and completely nonverbal.

Sometimes at night when she thought I was asleep, I could hear Becky's muffled sniffs and soft crying as she tried to stifle the sounds with her pillow. But inside, I knew she was dying as well.

Some children have physical handicaps and some are intelectually handicapped. Our son had both. And as he grew older, the gaps widened between what he could do and what typical children his age could do.

We had been holding on to the phrase developmentally delayed because of the implied meaning that he was simply delayed and would eventually catch up. But we could see that he was falling further and further behind other children his age.

My emotions rolled around like a pinball bouncing off everything. I experienced anger, grief, frustration, disappointment, despair, and an overwhelming feeling of being out-of-control.

I had hope on Monday and felt hopeless on Tuesday. Everything makes sense on Wednesday and nothing makes sense on Thursday. I felt like I could see clearly on Friday, but walked around in a deep, dense fog on Saturday.

But every morning, I would put on my fake smile and my plastic face for the world.

Some days I was so hypersensitive that everything seemed to set my emotions ablaze and the very next day I was just too numb to feel anything at all.

We had prayed and prayed over our son before he was ever born. We had asked God for a healthy pregnancy and a healthy child. Becky and I were both persons of deep faith and trust in God. We had faithfully believed in and fully expected a typical child. What had gone wrong?

Becky and I had both grown up in Christian homes and our faith was a vital component of our lives. Going to church on Sundays was a key part of our lives. At first, we would take Jon Alex with us to church and he could stay in the nursery with the other children.

As he grew older, though, his impaired intellectual challenges and cognitive damage made him fall further and further behind the typical kids his age. Then, when the autism began to manifest itself, his inappropriate noises, outbursts, sounds, and squeals would interrupt any attempt to sit through a church service.

At the most inopportune times, usually during a prayer or when the room was silent, my boy would announce his presence in his unique way to the rest of us! People would turn and I could feel their stares on my own face.

We tried to distract him by slowly feeding him bits of a bagel during church, primarily during the message. But as he grew, soon it was taking three bagels to cover the time and that still wasn't enough! I thought I was going to have to open an omelet bar in the back pew.

Every week, Becky had to take him out at some point in the service. They would end up waiting in the car until I joined them after service.

We reached the point where, for a season, we could no longer attend church as a family. We would alternate weeks of one of us staying home with Jon Alex while the other went to church alone. Church became one more symbol of frustration, bitterness, and despair in our lives.

Finally, in desperation, we hired one of Jon Alex's teaching assistants from his school and paid her out of our own pocket to come to church with us so she could attend to Jon Alex and take him out when necessary.

I was paying someone to come to church with us, just so my wife and I could go to church together. I felt like my son's special needs were not only robbing me of my dreams, my career, and my time, but also now my faith. I hated living in the upside-down world.

Chapter 3
ELEVEN WORDS THAT CHANGED MY LIFE

Our lives had become a sleepless blur as we tried to attend to all of our son's needs and treatments. Special diets, therapies, alternative therapies, his lack of any consistent sleep schedule, his behavior oddities, his constant needs—it was all taking an extreme toll on us physically, emotionally, and spiritually.

We tried to put on a brave face for each other. We tried to be strong and hopeful for each other, and in public.

Meanwhile inside, in the places in our hearts that we hide from everyone else, we were dying. Emotionally, mentally, spiritually, and relationally—we were dying.

I would lay awake at night searching, pleading, and still determined to find a solution. It was like trying to solve a special Rubik's cube that actually has no solution. Your mind twists, spins, plots, and searches for an answer that is never coming. You realize that, but you can't quit trying or searching.

Slowly, I started realizing that this child may never leave our care. As I wrestled with this thought, it absolutely overwhelmed me.

"Who is going to take care of my son when I'm gone? What will happen to him when I'm no longer alive to care for him?" It's the thought that keeps every special-needs dad awake at night.

I was struck with the thought *I have to live just one day longer than my child.* That became our goal—to live one day longer than our child.

Knowing that certain dreams I had for my life were never going to happen wrecked me. The plans, the goals, and the course I plotted for my life—everything was now going to be altered and affected.

I fought and wrestled with that notion with everything in me. I had made those plans, they were mine, and I did not want to let go of them willingly. I held on stubbornly, determined to still make it all work. I was angry that I was going to have to set those plans and dreams aside.

There was no reason here. And I certainly couldn't see what could possibly be the purpose or plan for this happening in our lives.

And then three short sentences changed my whole life.

Actually it was eleven simple words.

All those years of chasing answers. All those years I had searched for why this had happened and where was God. Here was the answer.

One night. Three sentences. Eleven words that changed everything for me.

My life would never be the same again.

Use whatever cliché you prefer—game changer, difference maker—all I know is it transformed my life forever. Eleven life-altering words.

"As he (Jesus) passed by, he saw a man blind from birth. And his disciples asked him, 'Rabbi, who sinned, this man or his parents, that he was born blind?' Jesus answered, 'It was not that this man sinned, or his parents, but that the works of God might be displayed in him.'" (John 9:1-3, ESV)

The words leaped off the page at me, especially the last eleven words.

"But that the works of God might be displayed in him."

What the disciples were asking Jesus was essentially the same question I had been asking. They had encountered a man who had been born with a disability. He had been born blind.

And, just like me, they had assumed someone must be at blame. Someone must be at fault or was being punished. They, too, were searching for an explanation or reason.

Here was Jesus himself saying this man had been born blind so that the works of God could be displayed in his life. This (the disability) had happened so that the works of God could be displayed. Some translations even say the "power of God" or "glory of God."

Was it possible that my son's special needs could really be part of God's plan to display his works and power through my son's life? Would God really allow this because he intended to use our circumstances in some greater purpose? Was God really intending to take this suffering and redeem it to demonstrate his great power and works? How is that even possible?

Because if that's true, then it truly does change my perspective on my son's disability.

Was my son's autism and cerebral palsy part of God's plan to bring glory and honor to him by somehow using my son's life in ways I could not fathom or ever imagine? Would God allow something to happen because what he wants to accomplish through it is far greater and more significant to his purposes?

I had to explore this idea further. God took me deeper into his word. I found my confirmation in the 139th Psalm where David, speaking of God, writes:

> *"For you formed my inward parts; you knitted me together in my mother's womb. I praise you, for I am fearfully and wonderfully made. Wonderful are your works; my soul knows it very well.*
>
> *My frame was not hidden from you, when I was being made in secret, intricately woven in the depths of the earth.*
>
> *Your eyes saw my unformed substance; in your book were written, every one of them, the days that were formed for me, when as yet there was none of them."* (Psalm 139:13-16, ESV)

I took my pen and underlined the words, "wonderfully made." Then I wrote in the margin, "Every day of life is recorded in God's book before we are ever born."

I was stunned.

God was declaring that my son was fearfully and wonderfully made just the way he was. And not only that, but God already knew what would become my son's life story. He had a plan for his life.

Slowly, the realization sunk in deeper.

I grabbed a legal pad and wrote the phrase that has become the cornerstone of our beliefs and the anchor of our hope.

"Wonderfully made ... created for a plan and a purpose ... destined to glorify God."

Those are the words we would choose to use in describing our son. The world would say of him that he was autistic or challenged, but we chose instead to say of him, "He is wonderfully made, created for a plan and a purpose, and destined to glorify God."

God had declared it, and I chose to believe it.

Yes, he was still afflicted with his cerebral palsy and his autism, but that's not how we defined him any longer.

God not only created him, but God created him in God's own image. God was decreeing that he was wonderfully made and that God himself had determined the plan for all the days of his life, and had written them down before Jon Alex was ever born.

To this day, I have a picture of my son on the wall beside my desk. Underneath the picture, I have John 9:3 written. As I go about my day, it's my ever-present reminder that my son was born this way so that God's work and power could be on display in his life.

There are some days I have to look at that picture just to lift my spirit out of the pit and remind me that God has a plan for all of this.

The scriptures further decree that *"And we know that for those who love God all things work together for good, for those who are called according to his purpose."* (Romans 8:28, ESV)

If we surrender our challenges and struggles to him, God's word says all things will work together for good, *according to his purpose.*

That last phrase is absolutely essential, because my definition of good and your definition of good can be far different from God's definition of good.

Likewise, God's purpose may be totally different from what I'd like his purpose to be. In fact, this side of heaven I may never know what his purpose is for my son's challenges.

That doesn't change the fact that God was going to somehow redeem our circumstances and use them for good. I recalled the story of Joseph from the Old Testament.

His brothers, who faked his death, had thrown Joseph into a pit. Then they sold him into slavery. He gets set-up, entrapped, falsely accused by his employer's wife, and thrown into prison. He is left to rot in prison for two years. His life literally crumbles around him and he has to struggle to find God's purpose in his suffering. But God used Joseph's troubles and redeemed the situation so that by the end of the story, Joseph was the second most powerful man of his country and reunited with his brothers and father.

The defining moment comes when Joseph boldly declares *"As for you, you meant evil against me, but God meant it for good..."* (Genesis 50:20, ESV)

God will take what is meant to harm you, and he will use it for good.

But it's our choice. It's all a matter of our perspective. As parents of a child with special needs, we have to make that choice every day, in every situation, and with every challenge.

I thought back to that night under the tree when God's Spirit had whispered, *"I have given you a blessing, what you do with it is up to you."*

God had told me then that this would be a blessing for me, but only if I chose to look at it that way. The choice is mine. And the choice is yours as well.

Am I going to look at this as a burden, or will I choose to look at this as a blessing? Are you going to look at your circumstances as a burden or a blessing?

Sometimes it is excruciatingly difficult to see what we are facing or walking through as a blessing. At times, I have to force myself to find anything positive or good.

If I'm honest, sometimes it just doesn't work too well. But with every opportunity to make the choice, it gets a little easier.

When I am determined to find the blessing in my circumstances, God opens my heart and mind and reveals things to me that I might have missed if I had closed my heart.

Is it a burden or blessing? It's up to you.

There is this big theological point often called "the sovereignty of God." Volumes and volumes of books have been written, discussed, and debated about the meaning of God's sovereignty.

The sovereignty of God means that all things are under God's authority and control, and that nothing happens without his direction, knowledge, or permission. He is aware of everything. God works all things according to his own will and purposes. Absolutely nothing takes him by surprise or catches him off guard. God has the power and right to govern all things, and does so without exception.

In a very simple but easy to understand manner, here is what I have concluded it means in my life. Everything in my life, good or bad, was either allowed to happen to me or given to me by God. This doesn't mean everything bad in my life is because God caused it. We do live with free will in a sinful, fallen world. But his sovereignty dictates that ultimately, his power supersedes all else, and his purposes are greater than my temporary circumstances.

God didn't get up off the couch one day to go get something out of the refrigerator, turn his back for an instant, and slap his forehead, saying, "Whoa! What happened? I turned my back for a moment and the Davidsons have a child with special needs? I sure didn't see that coming." Nothing catches God by surprise or off guard. My child with special needs was not an accident.

Sometimes I struggle with jealousy and envy of parents with only typical children. As hard as it is to grasp, I have to realize God has purposed my life to be the way it is. When I desire any life other than the one I have been given, in a way I'm blaming or second-guessing God.

I began to realize God had in fact given us a blessing. Jon Alex was a gift and we were the gift-keepers. God had entrusted us with a gift and now I had the choice whether to believe that or not.

God was not going to change my circumstances; God was going to walk through my circumstances with me. I needed to quit praying for God to remove the pain in my life, and instead surrender to him and ask him to use my pain and suffering for his glory. I did not need to ask him to change my circumstance; instead, I should ask him to go through the trials with me and teach me along the way.

Once I accepted that I had been given a gift, a blessing not a burden, my entire perspective changed. I had to decide if I was going to be a "why person" or a "how person." I think everyone is one or the other. And whether you are a "how" or a "why" person has enormous impact on everything you encounter in life, especially being the parent of a child with special needs.

"Why" people spend their lives wondering why everything in their lives happened. Why am I struggling with this? Why did that happen? They always feel victimized or as if someone is to be blamed. In this journey raising a child with special needs, the road to understanding "why" is a dead-end road. You will wander aimlessly in circles instead of climbing out of the emotional pit.

The pivotal choice is to choose to be a "how" person. "How" people respond to their challenges and trials by asking, "How can goodness come out of this situation? How can God redeem this and use it for his purposes? How can God be glorified by my response here? How can I rise above this?"

That shift in perspective changes everything in this walk. Now, everything made sense to me. God was telling his story through my life and my son's life. This was not to be our story, but rather his story. Through the telling of his story, he was teaching us about unconditional love, the abundance of grace, the essence of a gift, and the meaning of a selfless life.

I was going to learn that my joy is not dependent upon my circumstances. God had chosen me for this and called me with a plan and purpose for my life. My joy is dependent on where I am with Christ. If I try to place my joy in anything other than my relationship and standing with Christ, I will never find everlasting, unstoppable, un-quenching joy. I may find fleeting happiness, but not lasting joy.

I realized God was going to teach me so much about his own character and nature by calling me to be the dad of a son with special needs. God would use this experience to teach me so much about God himself, and my relationship with him.

God had indeed given me a most incredible blessing, a rare gift to be unwrapped.

God will do amazing and incredible things in our life and walk with him if we yield our circumstances asking him to use them instead of asking him to remove them.

"But that the works of God might be displayed in him."

Those eleven words led to a whole new understanding of my son's disability and God's plan for his life.

Chapter 4
THE STORYTELLER

Maybe it's because I grew up in a small rural town in the South.

Maybe it's because I share so many of the same values, morals, and ideals that the television show portrayed.

Maybe it's just because I love old-school comedy and quirky characters.

For whatever reason, I have always been, and still remain, an avid fan of the *Andy Griffith* television show. If I'm watching television and I come across an old rerun, I am probably going to stop and watch it to this very day.

My favorite character on the *Andy Griffith* show was Deputy Barney Fife, played by actor Don Knotts. The character of Barney Fife was a bungling, goofy, misfit of a Deputy Sheriff who owed most of his success to the sheriff's fixing of his missteps. The role was perfectly suited for Don Knott's slapstick, over-the-top comedy. In fact, he would win an Emmy Award for each of the five years he appeared on the show.

Don Knotts was so good in that role that it hurt his chances to become a serious actor. He was so typecast that most of his latter roles in television were playing very similar style characters. No one could see him playing a serious role in film or television.

Can you imagine Don Knotts as Don Corleone in *The Godfather*?

The wrong main character will ruin a good story. People were concerned that if they cast Don Knotts into a serious role, it would ruin the story.

God casts and directs his story the same way.

God is telling his story around us all the time, and he invites you and me to play a part in his story. And that's the part I keep forgetting. It's his story.

I'm not even the main character in the story of my own life. My life story, according to God, is about Jesus. I just get to play my little supporting role while Christ stars in the story.

I realized my son's life story was just the pencil that God was using to write God's own story. My son is his canvas and God is painting a magnum opus.

The story of your life is really God's story. You are playing the role he has assigned to you.

Sometimes I struggle with accepting the role God has given me in the telling of his story. Oftentimes I don't like the script. There are certain scenes in my life as a dad of a child with special needs that I would just soon leave out of the script altogether.

Don't you wish life came with a DVR and a remote control? So when the hard scenes in life happen, you could just push a button and skip ahead. Or you could hit a different button and just keep reliving a good moment in your life. Don't like what's happening in your life? Just press a button and skip ahead to a good time.

As I go further down this journey raising a son with special needs, I'm finding that the hard scenes I often want to skip are the ones that end up mattering the most in my life.

I have to remember that everything God does, he does to accomplish his purposes, and to bring glory and honor to his name. So my struggles become his stage. My trials become his triumphs. My weaknesses reveal his strengths. My responses show his glory.

The way I respond to my challenges in raising a child with special needs, the way I let God use my circumstances to accomplish his purposes, the way I react to the trials—it's all part of the way I tell my story. And the way I tell my story becomes the way I live his story.

God has given each of us a unique story when he created us. We cannot be envious or jealous of someone else's story. We can't try to live someone else's story. We also can't let someone else try to control our story.

When they film a television show or a movie, they don't film the scenes sequentially—meaning all the scenes that comprise the finished product aren't necessarily shot in the order they will appear in the story.

God's purpose for your life is like that. Some scenes don't make sense to us right now because we haven't seen the finished product. And this side of heaven we may never know the purpose, the point, or the reason for all we endure.

But we know God is creating a masterpiece, an epic magnum opus. We were chosen to play our part. Our responsibility is to make sure we are a story worth telling.

Once you realize that God has a plan and a purpose, you shift your perspective. It was really a conscious choice I had to make. Once I decided to choose joy and receive this as a blessing not a burden, I found a way to cope with my new normal.

So now I had come to the realization that my son was wonderfully made by God, created for a plan and a purpose, and destined to glorify God. I believed now God was going to tell God's story through our lives and display his power through my son. I accepted that I had been chosen and called. The only thing left was my choice whether or not to be committed.

"Don't you feel cheated about the life you imagined you and your son would have? Don't you feel like you have been robbed of so many blessings by having a child who can't talk, can't walk, and can't really do the things a typical child should be able to do?"

"Don't you feel robbed of all the activities a dad and a typical child get to do together?"

The questions come often. They are very valid questions actually. Usually they come from well-intentioned people who don't understand the perspective God has given me about raising a child with special needs. Sometimes, however, I do throw a pity party where I ask and answer the question of myself.

It's funny, though, that I get so defensive when other people ask the question. But sometimes when I allow myself to go to the Dark Side, I listen to that whisper in my own voice and it lures and beckons me.

If I'm not careful, I can let those thoughts into my head and they ruin me for a while. I can get down and depressed quickly and let the negativity of my circumstances steal my joy and rob me of my blessing.

I had an interesting conversation with a missionary to Central Asia one weekend. I asked him how I could pray for his area of the world. He said "Please don't pray for the persecution of Christians to end in our area. Pray that we would be able to endure it."

He explained that the biggest revelations of God, the biggest manifestations of God's presence, seemed to occur when the circumstances from the outside seemed the bleakest and most desperate.

I have discovered that to be true in my own life. Many of the hardest seasons or trials we have had to endure have resulted in the biggest manifestations of God's presence in our lives. Sometimes God must allow us to be wounded deeply in order to use us for even greater purposes.

I decided God was going to use this new life as a dad of a child with special needs to wreck me completely. He wanted to wreck me so that he could rebuild me into a much better model.

It made me think about all the time I have wasted asking God to remove circumstances in my life. Times I prayed for him to take away pain and suffering and eliminate things in my life. Instead, I should have been praying for endurance to persevere so I could experience the blessings that the situation would bring me. I should have prayed for him to teach me and reveal himself to me through the trials.

Looking back, every trial I have endured has been an incredible teaching moment where God has revealed so much to me about himself. I have to learn, as scripture teaches, to take each thought captive and line it up with the truth of God. If it doesn't line up, I need to reject the negative thought and not allow it into my head in the first place.

So I have a new answer now to the question of "Do you feel cheated?"

Yes, I do. My walk with a profoundly handicapped child has indeed cheated me of so many things.

I have been cheated out of having to worry about my son walking away from God. I have been cheated out of never comprehending God's unconditional love. I have been robbed of worrying that my son will make wrong decisions in his life. I have been cheated out of concern that the enemy will deceive him or lure him to walk away from God someday. I have been denied a life of never grasping God's mercy, God's strength, God's power, and God's plan for our lives together.

Cheated? Oh, yea. ...

But who's cheating whom?

Recently, we got Jon Alex's latest progress report from his school. Because he is in a Comprehensive Development Classroom (CDC), his progress report looks different from a traditional report card.

The report runs several pages long and lists in detail all the goals and skills they are working on with him. Then each entry gets a numerical score to indicate whether progress is being made and, if so, to what degree.

I use to cringe when the report came out. I knew what it would say. I dreaded it to the point that I quit reading it.

The entire process was just so depressing and demoralizing, seeing page after page of the same things mentioned over and over, along with notations of no progress being made.

Over the years, I've come to terms with it and can now accept it. As a parent of a child with profound developmental challenges, I've come to terms with a lot of things over the years.

My son will never excel at athletics. He will never be a scholar. He will never paint a masterpiece, solve complex math problems, write a novel, play a musical instrument, or score the winning basket.

I'm *okay* with all that now.

What I want for Jon Alex is for him to realize the love of Jesus Christ and then allow his life to be a mirror that reflects that love to others and draws them to Christ. In other words, just for his life to reflect God's glory in every way and point to Jesus.

That's what matters most. That's a life of true significance. That's the kind of life that changes the world.

And from the moment of his birth, I have seen God's hand on his life, giving him a plan, a purpose, and a destiny that glorifies God.

Meanwhile, you and I still struggle. We think we have to earn something, achieve something, or accomplish something. We measure our success in life by the size of our paycheck or house, by our title or career, by what we accomplish, build, or master. We compare our experiences to those of others on social media. We forget that when we are viewing social media, we are viewing that person's highlight reel, and that may not accurately reflect real day-to-day life.

Be honest, have you ever compared your life to others you know, or went to school with, or grew up with, just to see just how you measure up on the world's success scale?

And so we go on wasting our lives on things that just don't matter. I did this myself trying to self-medicate in coping with my son's special needs. The endless pursuit of misguided happiness drove my every action. Some people turn to alcohol, others to pills, inappropriate relationships, or other outlets as coping mechanisms to numb the pain.

For me, I threw myself into accumulating possessions. I put in a pool, bought a hot tub, drove the nicest SUVs, and remodeled our house. I traded cars every year and a half, and I tried to spend us out of the pain.

I hit rock bottom when I converted half of our basement into a man cave. I set it up with leather seating, a big screen TV, refrigerator, game table, foosball, and air hockey. I sprinkled all my sports memorabilia and souvenirs throughout the room. I was so proud of my monument to myself.

One night after the renovation was completed, as I sat in my new leather recliner flipping the channels on my big screen, all of a sudden, what I had done dawned on me.

I had built this awesome man cave in the basement.

Going down into the basement meant going down fifteen narrow steps to get there. My son, with his cerebral palsy, would never be able to come down there. Jon Alex would never be able to join me in my man cave. I realized I had built a monument to my own selfishness, greed, and needs.

I had built a false idol for me to worship. I fell on my knees and wept for what I had done and how I had been keeping score. I was determined to change my measures of success and how I kept score. Now I began thinking.

What if every one of us got up every day determined to do nothing else but receive the love of God, and then be a mirror that reflects his love to the world? What if we all said, "The only thing that matters at the end of the day is if I glorified God today"? What if that became the measuring stick for our definition of success?

What if?

I believe we would change the world one day at a time. We have to change the way we keep score in life.

God has chosen us and called us to a different life. We cannot compare our lives to our friends and family. We cannot allow ourselves to fall into the comparison trap. We realized that our lives were different. Not worse, just different. That's why I call our life "the new normal." Normal is what we say it is.

My wife's new normal goes like this in the morning: Every morning, she engages in a mad dash obstacle course to get our son up, cleaned, fed, medicated, dressed, and out the door. She's also packing up her briefcase and laptop for work, making our lunches, and then out the door she goes in a whirlwind.

One time her day began at 4:30 AM, when Jon Alex decided to wake us all up. Being unable to talk, he made it clear by his fussing and crying that his breakfast wasn't coming fast enough to his satisfaction. It was an extremely windy day in our town on top of that, and Jon Alex just doesn't handle wind. He freezes up, refuses to move, and even struggles to breathe properly when he feels strong winds against his body. So getting him to the car and then into school was an arduous ordeal to say the least.

On my way home, Becky called me on my cell phone and was pouring out her heart about the bad day she was having. And to make it worse, in the middle of our conversation, my phone battery died.

When I got home, I could tell the minute I walked in that it had been a long day.

A therapist at school had sent a note questioning how well Jon Alex was doing at home in a particular area of emphasis, because he wasn't demonstrating progress when she worked with him at school. That was the breaking point.

With all the therapies, special diet needs, the 24/7 care he requires, and the assistance he needs with every single thing in his life, sometimes we just feel overwhelmed. There is so much to be done and so little time to do it all. It can be so easy for parents of kids with special needs to feel guilty, inadequate, and completely mired down in their circumstances sometimes. You desire to do so much for your child, but there are only so many hours in a day.

I know sometimes my wife reaches her breaking point, just like we all do. This was one of those times.

That night, she used her pillow to muffle the sounds of her own crying. I know that night she sat in absolute exhaustion at the table unable to find the energy to even lift her head.

She was smiling on the outside to mask the fact that she was dying on the inside. I felt utterly helpless and devastated that I didn't know how to help her in that moment.

Sometimes you just feel like no one understands, can imagine, or even gets what your life is like.

That's when you have to remember that God captures your tears in a bottle. God hears your silent screams. And when you feel like no one understands your life, please know that he does. He has not left you or abandoned you. He has chosen you.

Before the beginning of time, God says all the days of your life were ordained and written down before one of them came to pass. And even though your walk in life and the journey you are on are so different and so challenging, you were chosen to receive the blessing of your child with special needs.

It isn't punishment. It isn't anything you did. It is an honor. And he chose you to receive the blessing. He will give you the strength, mercy, and power you need to persevere, because you were chosen to be his hands, his arms, his heart, his voice, and his face to your child with special needs. You are the very presence of God in your child's life.

Your child may not be able to make you a card or gift. They may not be able to hug you, talk to you, or even be able to express or acknowledge their feelings for you. Other moms and dads may receive much more tangible expressions of love than you'll ever receive.

Always remember. Just as you love your child unconditionally, God says he loves you with an everlasting love as well. You were chosen. Some days, that's easier to grasp and believe than on other days.

I'm writing these particular words on a Friday.

Someone today will leave a doctor's appointment and go home to "Google" the word autism.

Someone else will sit up in the hospital bed while the doctor explains a chromosomal disorder.

Someone will cry himself or herself to sleep tonight overwhelmed, discouraged, and sad.

Someone will tear up feeling like friends are abandoning him or her now that he or she has a child with special needs.

Someone is going to feel like no one understands his or her burden or feels his or her pain.

Someone is going to go to an Individualized Education Plan (IEP) meeting for the first time.

Someone else is going to clutch his or her head in despair trying to figure out how to pay for all the therapies and doctor's appointments for cerebral palsy.

Someone is going to sign the divorce papers because their spouse has checked out ever since the diagnosis.

Someone is going to have a breakdown in the grocery store when his or her child with special needs goes into a meltdown.

Someone is going to pull off the side of the road because his or her son is going into yet another seizure.

Someone is going to lament that his or her own family doesn't understand.

Someone is going to feel rejected, betrayed, and all alone.

Someone is going to feel like everything he or she trusted in, believed in, hoped in, and expected was all a lie or an illusion.

Today is Friday.

But Sunday is coming.

Two thousand years ago, another group felt like their world had been rocked upside down.

Everything they had believed, expected, and trusted in was wrapped up in one person. They had staked everything on this person. And now his beaten, exposed dead body was hanging from a wooden cross. He had died like a common criminal.

And when he died, a part of them died, too. A part of their dreams, expectations, faith, and plans for the future died.

It was Friday. But Sunday was coming.

The disciples did not know what was coming Sunday. They did not know that the dead could be brought back to life. They did not understand that the only way to receive the blessing, the gift, and the promise of Sunday was to endure the breaking on Friday.

A lot of us today are in the same boat. A part of us has died, leaving us hurt, betrayed, cold, discouraged, and confused. Something happened that we didn't plan for, expect, or even see coming.

This journey we are on as parents of a child with special needs is challenging, difficult, and even bewildering at times. We are not where we once were. And we are not where we will be someday. We are stuck in the meantime.

The meantime is a frustrating place to be. You can't see the shore in any direction. What do you do in the meantime?

Today may be your Friday. What do you do when your plans and dreams died on a Friday?

You have to pick yourself up and say to yourself, "It may be Friday, but Sunday's coming!"

The plan and purpose God has for you and your child, the destiny God has for your child with special needs—you may never realize them on Friday.

Never give up your hope and trust—because it may be Friday, but Sunday's coming.

It's no secret how many of our children with special needs are being raised by single female caregivers. It's no secret how we are losing the dads. It's no secret how so few of the dads who do stick around are actively engaged and involved in the lives of their child with special needs.

I have committed to living my legacies out in the life of my son right now. I'm working at living a legacy, not just leaving one. It's never too late to start. Make today the day you become more involved, more engaged, more active in finding ways to give of your time, your creativity, and your energy to your child with special needs.

Some people are still dealing with the grief, the anger, or the denial of what has been given to them. Some of you are still searching for someone to blame or a way to fix what has happened. Some of you may still be bewildered, confused, and in a fog.

I am reminded of a hospital stay with Jon Alex in the Epilepsy Monitoring Unit. He didn't understand why we were there. He didn't comprehend that it was for his own good. He didn't realize that it was part of the process to find healing. He didn't understand why he had to suffer like that. He didn't find any purpose in the situation. He didn't realize that I was allowing it to happen because of my deep fatherly love for him.

I struggled to look at him, suffering and in pain. I struggled because with everything in me I wanted to grab my son and rescue him. I wanted to pull him up into my arms and say, "That's enough! You don't have to endure this anymore!"

With one command I could have stopped it.

But sometimes dads have to allow pain and hurt in order to accomplish the greater purpose. Sometimes showing unconditional love means allowing conditional pain. God, as a Father, is no different.

You didn't plan for what is happening in your life. You would not have chosen this path in life, and you may not have been ready for this. But here you are, and you have a choice to make.

Chapter 5
CHOSEN AND CALLED

Most people don't choose to be parents of children with special needs. That's why God chooses them. They don't grasp why he chooses them, and for many, they don't understand why they were called and chosen for this life.

There is one person who can really tell you why you were chosen for this lot in life. That one person who can tell you is your child with special needs. That child could tell you.

The unconditional love, the sacrificial life, the willingness to do whatever it takes to fight for that child, to take care of that child, to lay down your life for that child. They see it. They feel it. They know it.

For all the parents of children who think no one understands your life: your child with special needs gets it.

You may not get a card for Mother's Day or Father's Day. You may not get any presents for Mother's Day or Father's Day. You may not get a kiss or a hug either. For you, it may just be another day.

But for your child with special needs … well, you're his or her everything. That's why you were chosen. Your child needs everything, and you are his or her everything.

And God knew only you could be that everything. God loves us. He captures our tears, he sings over us at night, he listens to our pleas, and he walks beside us. When you cry out in frustration, when you just want to give up, when you just don't know what else to do—he hears you and wants you to know that he knows.

He also knows something about laying down your life in sacrifice for someone you love.

You know that whole notion of sacrificing yourself for the sake of loving someone who doesn't show much love or appreciation back? God understands.

So many of our children with special needs are being raised by single female caregivers. If you ever want to meet a true genuine hero, meet one of these moms. So many of them are trying to balance work, sometimes two jobs, and home life. On top of that, many have typical children and a child with special needs both.

Imagine with me this story: A single mom comes home at the end of a long day. This happens too often in the special-needs community. She took her child with special needs to therapy, her typical child to her piano lesson, checked on dinner in the crock pot, and put yet another endless load of laundry in the washing machine.

After dinner, she did the dishes, administered the baths, tried to figure out where she could cut expenses to get $85 for the doctor's appointment on Friday, laid out tomorrow's clothes, read two bedtime stories, and wrestled with her nonverbal autistic child for three hours trying to get him to go to sleep.

Around one in the morning, she cried into her pillow and wondered how in the world she could go on any longer. In four hours, she will get up and do it all over again.

Day after day. Week after week.

There is never enough time to get it all done, and there is always too much month at the end of the money. And she always feels guilty that she's not doing enough and that she should do more.

Her ex-husband's no longer really involved. He mentally checked out long before he physically checked out. Two years after the diagnosis, he just simply gave up. He couldn't figure out how to engage with the child.

He wasn't ready to give up his own dreams and couldn't bring himself to realize that his life wasn't going to be the same as he had planned originally. So he walked.

All her friends will post pictures on Facebook of the gifts and the special cards and notes their children made on holidays or special occasions. She says to herself, "I don't really care," but something inside of her will die all over again.

For all of you who may not hear from anyone else ever, or receive any gift or recognition at all—I want to make sure you understand just how much you mean to this world. That distant clapping you hear is coming from heaven. That's where they are joining with me in giving you a standing ovation.

I admire you, I respect you, and I just want to affirm you. There is a reason God called you and chose you to be a special-needs mom. He gets it, too.

Now, think about this true story for a minute with me.

Never in her wildest dreams could she have imagined this would happen. It certainly wasn't the path she had planned out for her life.

When she initially got the news, she was stunned. This pregnancy wasn't expected in the first place after all. But to then get the news that this child wouldn't be typical … well, no one ever plans originally or even dreams of giving birth to a special child.

She had learned this baby wouldn't be typical while he was still in her womb prior to giving birth. But as she tried to comprehend what that meant, she struggled to grasp the whole picture.

She didn't realize how hard the early years would be for her and her baby as they tried to come to terms with their new normal.

She felt all alone and isolated. It was such a rare condition that she felt like no one else around her could possibly understand or relate to her experience. No one she knew had even heard of this happening before.

She worried she would lose friends. She worried her family would turn their backs as well. And she feared her husband would drown in denial, anger, and bitterness, like so many dads of special children.

What if he became another vacant dad? What if he couldn't figure out how to be engaged or involved so he just checked out?

On top of all that, there was a chance this new baby was going to die prematurely. More than likely, she would outlive her own son and have to watch him die.

Someone had told her that she was chosen. Someone had tried to convince her that God had a hand in this somehow. But that was hard for her to believe. How could God have really chosen her to be the mom of a special child?

Sounds familiar, doesn't it? We know and hear of special families who go through something like this all the time, don't we? Maybe you can relate to some of this in your own personal experiences.

If so, you certainly can relate then to Mary, the mother of Jesus. She is the mother of the special child I'm referring to in the story I just wrote.

Mary would have related to so many of you, and your thoughts, feelings, and emotions. After all, Mary was the mother of a special child herself.

That someone who told her God had chosen and called her? That someone was a personal messenger from God, an angel named Gabriel.

And he greeted Mary by saying, "Greetings most favored one, the Lord is with you."

Mary was chosen and called to be the mother of a very special child, the Son of God. God picked her and God found favor on her.

And what about you mothers and fathers of children with special needs? God has chosen you, God has called you, and you have found favor in him as well.

No matter how overwhelmed you get, no matter how often you despair, no matter how hard you struggle, no matter how intense your pain can be at times, you are favored.

Through the exhaustion, through the feelings of inadequateness, through the struggle to understand why—the fact remains that God chose you and called you.

One of the passages in scripture that really speaks to me is found in the Gospel of Mark chapter 4:35-41.

"As evening came, Jesus said to his disciples, 'Let's cross to the other side of the lake.' So they took Jesus in the boat and started out, leaving the crowds behind (although other boats followed). But soon a fierce storm came up. High waves were breaking into the boat, and it began to fill with water.

"Jesus was sleeping at the back of the boat with his head on a cushion. The disciples woke him up, shouting, 'Teacher, don't you care that we're going to drown?'

"When Jesus woke up, he rebuked the wind and said to the waves, 'Silence! Be still!' Suddenly the wind stopped, and there was a great calm. Then he asked them, 'Why are you afraid? Do you still have no faith?'

"The disciples were absolutely terrified. 'Who is this man?' they asked each other. 'Even the wind and waves obey him!'" (Mark 4:35-41)

I'm struck by several facts in this compelling story. First of all, Jesus obviously would have known that the storm was coming. Since he demonstrated that he had the power to end the storm just by speaking to it, he obviously could have done the same thing to prevent it from happening in the first place.

Jesus made the decision to allow the storm so that his works—the power of God—could be displayed. Second, Jesus was the one who put the disciples in harm's way. He made the decision for them to cross to the other side of the lake in the boat.

He chose the destination. He chose the course. He chose the path to the other side. If the disciples had been able to make the choice, they certainly wouldn't have chosen this part of their lives.

Jesus had chosen them, Jesus had put them in the boat, Jesus chose the destination, and Jesus allowed the storm.

The other thing you can't miss in this story is the fact that Jesus got in the boat with them.

He didn't send them into the storm on their own. He was right there with them on the journey. And when they were fearful and terrified by the storm in their lives, they called on him. When they called on him, he calmed the storm.

What does this story teach us as parents of a child with special needs? God chose us and put us in a boat we didn't choose. He put us on a journey of his choosing.

So when the storms in your life rage and the waves threaten to capsize you, remember who is in the boat with you! Jesus promises to stay in the boat with us. As long as you call on his name and ask for help, he won't let you capsize.

You may take on water, the waves may crash over you, but with Jesus, you will survive the storms. Stay in the boat! You can be soaked but not sunk.

He calms your waves.
He tempers your winds.
He stills your storms.

God's strength is perfected through our weakness. God says his power is made perfect when we are in the middle of struggles and circumstances that seem too big or strong for us.

We are always focusing on our strengths, aren't we? We always want God to use our strengths and show us our gifts. Did you ever stop and think that your weaknesses and limitations are actually gifts? Stop and realize God wants to use your weaknesses, limitations, and struggles just like he wants to use your strengths and gifts.

Your weaknesses and limitations allow his strength and power to be magnified in your life. Surrendering to his will and accepting your purpose is liberating and freeing. Your suffering becomes the stage for God's glory to be displayed in your life. Can I give you another example?

It was the one place where he could go and meet with God. The one place where he knew he would find God's presence and fulfill his own purpose.

In many ways, it was holy ground to him.

It was his tabernacle, his sanctuary, and his chosen meeting house of God. He needed answers, he needed clarity, and he needed to find assurances of the purpose for his life.

And so quietly, he slipped out of the room where he had been. Through the darkened streets and the crossing of shadows, he walked slowly to the little garden at the foot of the grove of ancient trees known as the Mount of Olives.

He was headed to the Garden of Gethsemane.

He was going because he needed to encounter God. He was going because he had been called and he had been chosen. He was going because he was committed.

That night in the Garden of Gethsemane, scripture describes Jesus as "anguished and distressed." He was "grieving to the point of death."

Three times he pleaded with God, asking if there was any other way to remove this "cup of suffering." He begged God, wondering if there was relief or any other way. And yet, he was obedient to his calling, saying "Father, let your will be done."

That's when heaven and earth collided.

Everything made sense and nothing made sense in the same moment.
He knew what his purpose was and yet wished it could happen any other way.
He felt the will of God and he felt abandoned by God.
He felt the closest to God and the furthest from God in the same moment.
He felt like he was in the hand of God yet so far from God.
He claimed his purpose but it didn't erase the pain.
Confusion and yet clarity.
Torment and yet triumph.
Sorrow and yet joy.
Surrender and yet victory.
And then finally, he felt peace.

He felt a deep abiding peace that comes from knowing that he had found his purpose and his meaning.

We, too, have to come to a place of knowing and surrendering to God's will and then accepting what we were created to do.

The pains, torment, despair, and anguish in the Garden of Gethsemane surrendered to God to become a stage for the glory of God to be displayed. There, in that moment, we realize that God was in it all along. Victory is won by surrender.

The moments we feel the furthest from God are the very moments we are closer to him than we ever thought.

My son with special needs is my Garden of Gethsemane.

He is where heaven and earth collide in my life. His special needs have been my sorrow and my joy. He is where my mourning has been turned into dancing.

He has brought me the closest to the presence of God in my life at the same times I felt God was the furthest from me.

He is where clarity has been birthed out of confusion.
He is where I found the will of God for my life.
He is where I discovered my purpose and why I am on earth.
My pain is so deep, but my purpose is deeper.
He is where I am my weakest and yet I am my strongest.
He is where I have been wounded greatly, but healed deeply.
He is where I realized I have been chosen and called.
He is where I stand surrendered to God's plan.
He is where I go to find God's presence and hear his voice in my life.
The pain and suffering of this challenge surrendered for the stage of God's glory.

Finding your purpose doesn't erase your pain. But though your pain is deep, your purpose is even deeper. Dig deep.

Gethsemane means, "oil press." It's where the olives would be squeezed to extract the goodness of the oil inside of them.

My son with special needs is my oil press, squeezing the goodness and fruit in my life out of me.

He is my meeting house of God.

He is my Garden of Gethsemane.

Raising a child with special needs has taught me something else about myself. I've learned that it is OKAY to not be OKAY. What I mean is that as a parent, you sometimes feel so out-of-control and so helpless. If you are not careful, you begin to beat yourself up, constantly asking, "Am I doing enough?" You feel a constant pressure to put up this plastic wall that hides the pain and frustration and insecurity.

Between all the therapies, doctors, and dietary intervention, we found ourselves slipping into a feeling that it was never enough. We would put enormous pressure on ourselves feeling, "There is more we can do, there has to be more."

The reality is that there is always more you can do. But I had to realize that my calling to be a father meant that when my son was around me, sometimes he needed me to be a dad, not another therapist.

One of my biggest regrets at this point in our journey together, now that my son is sixteen, is that I didn't treasure those moments of just being a dad enough in the early years because of my obsession to fix this challenge.

When I counsel young dads just coming to terms with a diagnosis or just beginning to walk down this journey, I always tell them to savor the moments to just be a dad and enjoy those moments free of obsessing over the future, or wondering if you should be doing something more therapeutic to help your child.

Sometimes we struggle feeling we aren't worthy or equipped for this journey. We lament that surely God could have found someone else better gifted and more suitable to be a parent of a child with special needs.

We wonder deep inside what makes us worthy? What are we doing here? That's when we have to remind ourselves that it is God's grace that sustains us. God's grace empowers us. God's grace deems us worthy of our calling. It is only by his grace. Allow me to demonstrate that grace in this next story.

"Wait a minute. What's he doing here? Why is he even allowed in the room, much less at the table?"

The question had to be asked the first time the King summoned the royal family to the dining table. The true sons and daughters of the King exchanged looks, whispered back and forth, and looked curiously on the late-arriving guest.

How can he possibly deserve to be here at the King's table? they thought silently. The King himself, knowing what they must be thinking, announced, "Mephibosheth will always eat at my table."

King David had made a pact with his friend Jonathan before a brutal civil war that if anything happened to either one of them, the other would take care of his surviving family.

There was only one member of the family left, a man named Mephibosheth, who had special needs, being crippled in both his feet.

From the moment David learned of Mephibosheth, he adopted him into his family, gave him back his inheritance, and invited him to have a seat at the King's table.

"And David said to him, 'Do not fear, for I will show you kindness for the sake of your father Jonathan, and I will restore to you all the land of Saul your father, and you shall eat at my table always.'" (2 Samuel 9:7, ESV)

That's one of my favorite passages. I use it often in my speaking to demonstrate how God's (the King's) table includes seats for those with special needs. I use the illustration to proclaim that we are all welcome in God's Kingdom (the table), even those with special needs. I love to use this story when speaking to churches about opening their doors and their programs to include those with special needs and disabilities.

Recently, in preparation for presiding over the Lord's Supper at my own church, I was rereading the scriptural account of the Lord's Supper. As I read the account again, it mentions that Jesus was there with all twelve disciples. All twelve? Something struck a nerve inside me, causing me to blurt out the same thing the King's kids did in my previous story.

"Wait a minute. What's he doing here? Why is he even allowed in the room, much less at the table?"

I was referring to Judas. Jesus knew full well what Judas was about to do. He even announced it as they dined around the table. Yet,

Jesus still took bread and wine, blessed it, gave thanks, and served it to Judas.

Myself there is no way I could do that. I wouldn't even have allowed Judas in the room, much less at the table.

Oh, the unbelievable grace of our Lord!

I felt like the Spirit of God prompted me, though, to take another look around the table, as if saying, "Look around again."

This time, I noticed Peter. Just a few hours after the supper, Peter would deny even knowing Christ three times. Jesus had even warned Peter at the table that, *"This very night—before the rooster crows, you will deny three times that you even know me."* (Matthew 25:36)

"Wait a minute. What's he doing here? Why is he even allowed in the room, much less at the table?"

How in the world could Jesus allow Judas and Peter to sit at his table, and even serve them, knowing how they were going to betray him?

Then I felt the Holy Spirit thumping in my soul and prompting me, "Take one more look around the table and tell me what else you see."

This time I looked around the Lord's table—and I began to weep and cry. This time, I saw myself at the Lord's table.

Me. With all my hang-ups, missteps, baggage, doubts, and faults.

Me. With all my sins, my issues, and my garbage in my heart.

I was sitting at the King's table.

"Wait a minute. What am I doing here? Why am I even allowed in the room, much less at the table?"

God reminded me that just like Mephibosheth, I too am broken, and crippled in my own way. We all have our own special needs. And like Mephibosheth, I too have been adopted into his royal family and given an inheritance.

And just like Mephibosheth, because of God's unquenchable grace, you and I will always have a seat at the royal table and dine with the King.

Chapter 6

THE GIFT AND THE GIFT-KEEPERS

Jesus replied, "Anyone who drinks this water will soon become thirsty again. But those who drink the water I give will never be thirsty again. It becomes a fresh, bubbling spring within them, giving them eternal life." (John 4:13)

She waited to leave home until she was sure most people had already returned home from getting the day's food and drink needs. Given her circumstances, going out in public was just something she found difficult and awkward to do.

She was embarrassed, and yet hated herself for feeling that way. She would have been perfectly happy to just stay in her isolated home and avoid the crowd altogether. They pointed at her as they whispered behind her back. They muttered and gossiped.

Her home was her safe haven. Her home was where she felt the least vulnerable and the most protected. But her home was also her prison.

Her life circumstances made her different from the others. As a result when the other women would engage socially, laughing and talking as they went about their daily chores, she sat home by herself and waited. She didn't feel they would really understand or grasp her situation. It made her feel like an outcast. She hadn't planned on her life turning out this way, but it had happened. The challenges and the trials had taken a toll on her.

So she was waiting. Waiting for enough courage to leave. Waiting for the right moment. Waiting until she felt it was safe. Waiting until no one else was around to notice. Waiting until she didn't have to look anyone in the eye.

But mostly she was waiting for hope. Waiting for someone to make sense of all this to her. Waiting for an explanation of how this could possibly be God's choosing for her life. Waiting for someone to please show her meaning, significance, and fulfillment given the challenges and circumstances of her life. Waiting for someone to tell her how to find sense and joy despite her difficulties.

"Is this all there is to my life?" she may have wondered. "Is this as good as it gets? What good could ever come out of this experience?"

Have you as a parent of a child with special needs ever wondered that yourself? Have you ever felt like the woman in the story I just detailed? Have you ever cried for an explanation from God or searched for meaning in this journey as a parent of a child with special needs? Have your struggled with your role in the story of your life?

Seeing by the sun that the time was right, she slipped out with her bucket and headed to the well. At that moment, she realized that her soul was thirstier than her body. And she ached to quench that never-ending thirst.

All the other people drew their water from the well in the early morning hours. So as she carefully approached the well in the noontime heat, she was startled to see a strange man sitting beside the well.

She averted her eyes, preferring to do her business quickly and concisely. She didn't want him to speak to her and she certainly didn't expect him to initiate a conversation with her.

"Will you give me a drink?"

She looked up and blinked rapidly. "Was he talking to me?"

He looked her right in the eyes. Nobody ever did that to her. Nobody ever searched her eyes and soul like this stranger. She glanced away in shock and defensively blurted out the first thing to come to her mind, "Why are you asking me for a drink?"

"If you knew the gift of God and who it is that asks you for a drink, you would have asked him and he would have given you living water," the stranger said.

"If you knew the gift..." The words echoed in her mind.

"If you knew the gift..."

"I have given you a blessing...."

"If you knew the gift," said the voice of God to the woman at the well in the fourth chapter of John.

"I have given you a blessing," said the same voice of God to the dad at the creek by the willow tree sixteen years ago.

Sixteen years later, I can say that this unexpected journey as a special-needs parent has been excruciatingly difficult, brutally hard, and incredibly draining. It's been more challenging than I could have ever realized.

But it's also been an incredible blessing and an amazing gift.

There is living water for all of us. Drink furiously and lustily of his water and never thirst again.

I beg you to stop by the well and drink today. Drown the fear within you, and embrace the gifts before you.

"What if he has an autistic moment in the middle of the store and people stare?"

"What if his vocal sounds and his rocking in his chair disrupts the others?"

"What if it's crowded and I'm trying to push a wheelchair and a shopping cart at the same time?"

"What if all the handicapped parking places are already taken?"

My wife was debating whether to engage in a game of Walmart Roulette with our son.

Normally she tries to avoid places like Walmart when she has our son with profound special needs accompanying her. But this time, the items she needed required a trip to the superstore here in our small town.

Fear was whispering in her ear though, and doubts were slipping in through the unlocked door to her heart. Taking a child with autism and cerebral palsy into such an environment would require staring down the coward within.

Navigating my son's wheelchair and a shopping cart simultaneously with the skill of a NASCAR driver, she made her way down the narrow, packed aisles.

That's when she saw them.

Two developmentally disabled young adults, with their caregivers, were in the produce department.

As she passed by, one of the young men began to demonstrably wave and gesture towards her. He approached her and my son, trying to communicate.

Garbled, nonsensical words and sounds gushed forth as the young man gesticulated wildly. His caregiver approached him from behind, and tried to explain and apologize.

My wife waved the caregiver off at the pass and flashed him an "It's okay, I'm safe" motion. For the next couple of moments she engaged and interacted with this intellectually challenged young man as if they were life-long friends.

"He is trying to tell you he likes fireworks, and wants to know if your son likes fireworks as well," explained the caregiver, pointing to my own teenage son in his wheelchair.

Soon Becky moved on to finish her shopping and waited in one of the checkout lines. As she moved steadily closer to the holy grail of finally paying for her items and exiting the store, a moment ordained in heaven unfurled right at the counter.

The challenged young man and his caregiver were across the aisle from her, checking out with a different cashier. The young man made eye contact with Becky and began to wave.

As she waved back and flashed him that dazzling smile I first noticed 24 years ago, he left his caregiver's side and walked over to where Becky and Jon Alex were.

He stopped right in front of my wife and gave her a big, yet tender hug, gingerly wrapping his arms around her and just holding her for a second.

No doubt the moment had been God-breathed, God-inspired, and God-ordained. Sitting in the car, tears in her eyes, Becky thanked God for that holy moment.

A moment where fear was trounced, the coward within defeated, and where grace was allowed to not only abound, but to triumphantly be displayed.

"I needed that moment," she would tell me later. "That was God's gift to me. If I had let the fear win, I would have missed something beautiful."

She did need that moment. But she was only partly right.

We all needed that moment.

The young man needed it. His caregiver needed it. The cashier needed it. Everyone in the store who witnessed the encounter needed it.

That was God's gift to all of us.

Because that is what God does. He takes broken vessels and he creates beautiful gifts that he uses to reveal himself to us. God creates nothing but masterpieces. Sometimes, you'll find one, even at Walmart.

When you feel the darkness threatening to engulf you, when you feel discouraged, when you feel all alone and desperate for a glimpse of hope, when the hurt won't go away and the weariness overcomes you, drink deeply from his well and quench your thirst.

I love to sit and watch Jon Alex when he is unaware of my presence.

I love to watch his facial expressions and mannerisms. Sometimes I feel like I catch a little bit of myself in him. I can tell when he is about to smile or laugh before he actually does.

I know everything about him. His blue eyes, his hair color that has recently darkened, his broken tooth, and his birthmark right below his waistline on the right side—I know all that.

I know he likes to sleep on his side, I know that his eyesight is poor, his feet are crippled, and his hearing is overly acute. I know all that.

That's not surprising, though—after all, I am his dad.

I watch his eyes dart around taking in his surroundings and the people around him. He doesn't say anything but I know him well enough to know what he is thinking.

I can tell by the way he is acting, his expressions, and his movements what he needs or wants, even though he doesn't speak.

Sometimes he doesn't even know I'm in the room with him. I treasure those moments. Like when I slip into his room at night when he is asleep. I'll just watch him sleep and listen to him breathe. Then I'll whisper a blessing over him.

When he gets mad or frustrated at his circumstances, I feel the pain inside him. I hurt for him and just want to reach out and console him and tell him how much I love him and what he means to me.

I know he doesn't understand why his path through life is so different, why it's such a challenge for him. I do. But it's hard to explain it to him right now. So I just hope he trusts me. His life has a purpose and a destiny.

I love him unconditionally. I always will. He's my son.

Those very words could also be God talking about me as his son. I believe God loves to slip into my presence when I'm not even aware. I believe he delights in all of his creation, of which I am a part.

Just as I know everything there is to know about my son intrinsically, I believe God knows me and knows my son the same way. The 139th Psalm speaks of God watching our frame as it was knit together, and of his eyes watching our unformed bodies.

Sometimes Jon Alex has this look on his face like he sees things we don't see. He tilts his head to the side and grins softly, as if heaven is playing a song just for him. He twirls his fingers to the music.

Early in the morning, I can hear him over the monitor making sounds and expressions none of us can understand. I wonder if he is talking to God in a language only the two of them can understand.

Sometimes I think Jon Alex sees angels. Sometimes I think he hears the music coming from heaven's chorus. Sometimes I think he talks to God … and God talks back to him. Sometimes I get jealous of his world.

Oftentimes we describe our children with autism as living in their own world.

Their senses are overly acute in many instances to touch, sound, sights, smells, and the tactile evidence of the world around them. And they can seem far more interested in their world than in ours. Maybe they really aren't living in their own world. Maybe they are living in the world as it was originally created.

My son Jon Alex lives in a world of unconditional love and acceptance. In his world, grace abounds, loves triumphs over all, and contentment can often be found with the simplest of things. His world is one of purity, simplicity, innocence, and goodness.

I'm jealous of his world. His world isn't polluted by envy, jealousy, pride and hatred. His world is enticing.

Maybe we are the ones living in our own little world.

Have you ever been mesmerized by children with autism and wondered what they were thinking, or what was going on in their minds? Have you ever looked at them and wondered if they were thinking the same thing about you?

When you have been puzzled by their behavior or baffled by their routine, have you ever wondered if they feel the same way about your behavior or routines? When you have struggled with their personality traits that can seem peculiar, have you ever wondered if they feel the same way about some of your personality traits that seem so peculiar to them?

Maybe we are the ones living in another world.

I know I have learned far more about the nature and character of God from my son than he has learned from me.

Doesn't surprise me when I think about it. After all, I suspect he talks to God a lot more than I do.

All those mornings at 4:00 AM when I hear my son making sounds over the monitor, the only person up that early is God anyway. I guess they like to hang out together in their world.

Caleb is a young man with autism in my son's classroom. I call him Jon Alex's wingman. They've become buddies over the years, walking down the same path in life together.

My son Jon Alex is completely nonverbal. Caleb does have a few words and some limited language, but mostly sounds. Sometimes, even though the rest of us don't understand them, they communicate together in a way only they understand.

I'm convinced one day they will write a tell-all book together and discuss what they've learned from riding in the backseat together.

When something isn't right in Caleb's world, he will shake his hands vigorously and say, "Fix it, daddy."

Often, no one knows what has got him so upset, but something has clearly triggered him into repeating over and over, "Fix it, daddy."

One time, Caleb's mom told him how sick Jon Alex was and that he was in the hospital. Together, Caleb and his mom prayed, "Fix it, daddy." When I heard about the prayer, I cried because I knew God had heard that sincere prayer from the heart.

I was pretty sure that all heaven stopped in silence and leaned towards earth to hear Caleb, praying for his little friend, "Fix it, daddy."

Books have been written on prayer. Countless books, essays, teachings, and sermons have been produced on faith. For hundreds of years, theologians have debated prayer, faith, and God's interaction in our world.

Caleb doesn't read those books. Caleb doesn't know any theologians. Caleb knows God.

And that's all Caleb needed to know. So Caleb turned his head towards heaven and asked his Daddy, "Fix it."

I remembered this when I broke my right foot. Actually, I broke it in several places. I went to see an orthopedist who took x-rays, examined my foot, and then proclaimed that for this type of injury, there is just not a whole lot that can be done.

A medical condition I have caused it and from his standpoint, there wasn't really any way to fix it. My best option was to learn how to live and cope with it, and hope for the best.

The foot was permanently deformed, as the bones would just haphazardly fuse back together on their own.

Faced with that prospect, I decided to seek out an expert specialist and have him take a look. So I made an appointment with a foot and ankle surgeon at a well-known medical university hospital for an evaluation. I went in and had the foot examined, and a whole new series of x-rays were made.

While I waited for the surgeon to come in and give me his opinion, I must admit to a certain amount of fear and trepidation. What if I do have to deal with this condition all my life? What if there is nothing that can be done? What if this is hopeless?

When the surgeon came in, we exchanged pleasantries for a few minutes, and then he got right to the point.

"Your foot is an absolute mess. It's a wreck. But I can fix this. I know how to treat this and we're going to fix your foot for you. That's what we do. It won't be easy, but I deal with this all the time and I can take care of it."

All of the apprehension, fear, worry, and dread just drained off me. In an instant, I felt so much relief knowing it wasn't hopeless, that it could be fixed.

That started me thinking. So many times we make a mess of things in our lives that need fixing. But we buy into the lies that it's hopeless, that we just have to learn to live with it.

And so we go on feeling like our life is too messed up and that nothing that can be done. We keep going, trying to do life, while holding onto conditions from which we could find release and healing.

Conditions like guilt, shame, anger, bitterness, fear and anxiety, jealously and depression weigh us down.

Or we think our lives are just too broken to be fixed.

All the time we are doing this, God is sitting there saying to us, "I can fix this. This is what I do. No matter what the condition of your life, no matter what is broken—I can fix you. I deal with this all the time. In fact, it's my specialty. Please let me fix this for you."

But it's up to us to make an appointment to go see the Great Physician. I happen to know his office is open twenty-four hours a day, seven days a week. He never closes.

Go ahead and call him today. You don't have to keep living with it one more day.

Tell him, "Fix it, Daddy."

One of my biggest struggles as the dad of a son with profound special needs is jealousy. After sixteen years, you would think I would be capable of rising above it, but it still strikes from time to time.

This time of year as I write this is especially hard. Our son's disabilities preclude us from taking any kind of vacation or time off to relax and renew. He simply can't travel, and the need for constant care just makes it too difficult for us to attempt.

With our school year coming to a close, I get envious of other's vacation plans. Hearing of upcoming beach trips and such are difficult for us, if we are being transparent. I loathe Facebook during this time because I get so jealous of everyone else's posts and pictures from their wonderful trips and vacations.

It's very easy for a special-needs parent to get so envious of typical parents posts on social media. That's when you have to remind yourself that you cannot compare your life to everyone else's lives.

Then there is the whole end of the school year process. There are talent shows, award ceremonies, graduations, parties, and proms. These can be another reminder of awards my son will never win, talents he will never have, and so many other typical experiences that his walk in life will not include.

Every time someone tells me their child is in a gifted program at school, I always reply with, "My son *is* the gift."

His and our whole world turned upside down the summer he moved to high school. His middle school had a ceremony for the eighth grade student body graduating middle school and moving on to high school.

In all honesty, we didn't want to attend the ceremony. Jon Alex would be wheeled through the alphabetical line to give him a certificate of achievement, but cognitively it wouldn't mean anything to him. So we had some hesitation about even attending.

I was afraid that in front of the entire student body, someone might shout something hurtful or derogatory when his name was announced. My biggest fear was that someone in the crowd would mock him or embarrass him.

You hear and read so much about bullying in schools. You see the stories, and as a dad of a child with special needs, deep down you fear your child may be a target.

So we went to the ceremony and attended the program. The teachers and staff went through a long list of superlatives and award winners.

My son attended Algood Middle School and the school nickname and mascot is Redskins.

At the end of the awards presentation, my son's teacher came to the podium and she began to describe the winner of this year's Redskin Award.

She described a young man who everyone knows and loves, who is the kindest and happiest boy in the school. All of a sudden, I saw my son's aide begin to wheel him up to the podium … and I knew.

I knew and I cried. I cried because the entire student body, parents, and faculty stood up to give my son a standing ovation. I wept with pride and joy and actually dropped the camera.

In that one moment, my son won the Super Bowl, the Masters, and was named the World Series MVP. In that one moment, my son was elected president of the United States, won the Nobel Prize, and walked on Mars.

And then I had to repent. Not for my pride did I repent.

I repented because, as a parent of a child with special needs, I had grown weary and jaded. I had assumed and imagined the worst might happen. I had misjudged my son's peers and others. I had braced myself for another disappointment and disillusionment.

I had never imagined or dared to dream of this.

What a reminder that goodness does still exist in this world! What a reminder that grace and dignity is still offered in this world. What a reminder that the next generation, despite what you hear, does care and still values virtues.

It was a reminder that acceptance and inclusion are not just terms in a book, but a real life code capable of being followed. Every life God creates has significance. I had confused accomplishment with significance. I had confused accomplishment with influence.

Here was my son's God-given plan and purpose on display before me. His life has significance and his life has influence.

He is the gift and I am the gift keeper. All those years I spent trying to find the perfect gifts for my son while in reality, he was the perfect gift. I remember those early days searching in vain for gifts to entertain my son.

Putting the mini roller coaster in the basement was probably a bit over the top.

I sat it up next to the giant ball pit across the basement from the animated rocking horse and the large swing hanging from the basement rafters. All we lacked was a dancing elephant and I could have charged for admission.

Yes, I had turned our basement into a kid's carnival. It was all part of the ongoing search to find the perfect toys to entertain my son when he was much younger.

A lot of dads try to relive their own childhood by purchasing toys for their toddlers based upon what reminds the dad of his own childhood, or what he envisions he would have liked as a child. I would search endlessly high and low to try to find toys that he would play with and that he would actually be able to enjoy. His disabilities created quite the challenge in that endeavor.

Before he was born, I had dreams of throwing a football together, shooting baskets, and playing games in the backyard. That had been my childhood with my dad, and I anticipated it would be the same with my son.

Now I was frustrated with trying to find gifts or activities to engage my son. His physical limitations and detachment caused by his autism made it difficult. One night, I sat there just swinging him in a platform swing that hung from the ceiling.

All of a sudden, I made the sound of a racing car going by us.

He cackled.

I made sounds of a fighter jet, a spaceship, and a fire truck roaring by us.

He smiled. He laughed. He giggled. He flashed me a gap-toothed grin.

Then he reached out and hugged my neck.

I began to cry.

In that moment, my son had taught me one of the most important lessons about parenthood.

Joy can be found in the simplest of things. Contentment can be found with just a few things. Happiness can be found in the small things.

As a dad, it is not about what activity you do or what gift you give your child. The real gift is simply taking the time to do something with your child.

Now that I am little bit older, I see that what matters most to our children is that we as dads are simply there, actively involved and engaged. The time spent together trumps any gift or present we may ever give them. We have to find creative ways to engage and be involved with our children.

I struggled at first to find ways myself. The frustration would grow and the futility mounted with every year. We would spend hours online and in stores searching for the perfect Christmas gifts for our son. I wanted something we could play with together.

But what in the world do you get for a child who is both intellectually and physically challenged? What gift seems right for a boy afflicted by cerebral palsy, autism, and seizures, who, even though he is a year older every year, is still a toddler in so many ways?

Finding toys to engage him that he would actually play with seemed futile. And believe me, we tried everything. I think I vicariously relived my own childhood by purchasing for him everything I imagined I would have wanted as a little boy.

It's part of the reason Christmas is hard on special-needs families in so many ways. One of the ways we don't talk about much, but we feel despair over so often, is in finding appropriate gifts for our kids with profound special needs.

My son has watched the same *Wiggly Safari* video featuring the Wiggles and the late Steve Irwin every day before dinner for eleven years. Every time he watches the video, it's as if he were seeing it for the first time. He laughs, he cackles, he roars. By the sounds he makes, I think in his own way he is singing along.

Finding other things he enjoys as much has proven futile. He has a few videos, some music CDs, and a couple of music toys, and seemingly no interest in much else. It is as if he is saying, "What else do I possibly need?"

The one thing he really needs, the one thing he has to have—he has already received.

Every morning his mother gets him up, cleans him up, fixes his breakfast, and dresses him. Then she takes him to school before heading off to work herself. After work, she cooks his meals, washes his clothes, changes his sheets, bathes him, and prepares him for bed.

Because of his needs and limitations, he requires 24/7 care for everything in his life. He is not capable of taking care of himself, and never will be. She is his world. She is his lifeline. She is his everything.

She is also exhausted. She is weary. She is overwhelmed and teetering on the edge half the time. There is too much to do and too little time and resources to do it all.

Sometimes she wonders where the strength will come to get up in the morning and do it all over again. She doesn't realize it, but she has given her child the perfect gift already. The only gift that would work. She has given herself.

She gets up every day and lays down her life for her child. Her dreams, her plans, her needs, and her life—she lays them down for his sake.

Because the only way he lives, is if she dies ... to herself ... every day.

Each and every one of you caring for an individual with special needs is doing the same thing. And by doing so, you are embodying the essence of the Gospel without realizing it.

The essence of the Gospel is God giving us himself. Spiritually, emotionally, and physically, we are dependent upon God for everything, just like your child is completely dependent upon you for everything.

God's perfect gift to us was the gift of himself in the form of Jesus. When God gives you a child with special needs, in essence, he is saying here is the embodiment of the Gospel. This child needs you just like you need God!

No other gift was suitable. No other gift could give us what we needed. We needed the gift of life.

God gave us himself in the form of Jesus, who would give up his own life to save ours.

And you as a special needs parent give your life up in a different way, but for the same reason, to save your child.

Don't beat yourself up trying to find the perfect gifts for your children with special-needs.

You have already given it to them.

Every day.

As a dad of a son with special needs, I also now realize the best gifts are sometimes the ones you didn't expect or think you would have wanted.

The reality is that our children themselves are the real gift. I believe my son with profound special needs is wonderfully made, created for a plan and purpose, and one of the most amazing gifts I have been given. He is the real gift. I am just the gift-keeper.

Chapter 7
NO MORE PEANUT BUTTER SANDWICHES

There is a choice to be made and you are the one who gets to make the choice. Choose wisely because every aspect of your life will be completely decided, affected, and determined by which choice you make and the perspective you take.

Make the right choice and God will use your struggles, challenges, and trials in life to bring you unspeakable joy and gratitude in all things. Choose wrongly and you will wallow in negativity, never finding the purpose or meaning in your life.

The choice is the difference between choosing life or death emotionally and mentally.

I have to constantly remind myself to choose joy and thankfulness. I have to constantly make the decision, even when it seems impossible, to find the joy and something in my situation for which to be thankful.

Raising a child with special needs is either a burden or a blessing. And in every moment throughout the day, I have to make that choice again and again.

Peter Pan … in case you wonder later in the next story.

When I was in elementary school, our school system started a gifted program for certain students who demonstrated exceptionality in science and math. I guess they needed to fill a spot for a freckled boy with bangs because somehow I was chosen to participate.

Each of us had to come up with a project idea to work on for the class. My peers quickly went about developing incredible projects worthy of the gifted program. But while they developed alternative forms of energy, created new ecosystems, solved complex math formulas, and sought world peace, I went down a different path.

I decided to conduct a blind taste test of peanut butters to determine which one was favored by my fellow fifth and sixth graders. I dipped spoons into jars of various brands and had my peers sample them blindfolded, choosing their favorite.

You see, I loved peanut butter. I still do. So my dream project was to spend my days working with my chosen medium, peanut butter. Which explains why now, some thirty-five years later, I still have never been nominated for a Nobel Prize.

When I was a toddler, my parents took me to the circus. When the ringmaster asked rhetorically if anyone knew any magic phrases, I stood up and shouted "A la peanut butter sandwiches!" because I had heard the Amazing Mumford do that on *Sesame Street*.

If you ask any connoisseur of peanut butter sandwiches, we will tell you there's a fine art form involved in making the perfect peanut butter sandwich. And it all begins by making sure you use ample peanut butter and spread it all the way to the very ends of the crust, covering the edges completely with generous amounts of gooiness.

Otherwise, you end up with a lot of worthless, spreadless crusts of bread when you are finished.

Why am I sharing my obsession with peanut butter with you?

Because five years ago, I died on a hospital table.

My body, overrun with a devastating toxic buildup, went into respiratory arrest and I quit breathing. Within minutes, I was placed on a ventilator to breathe for me, and I spent the next few days on life support in a medically induced coma.

A few weeks later, I returned home a complete invalid. I required 24/7 care with everything from feeding, bathing, medical care, even moving. I spent months in a wheelchair learning to walk again. For weeks, I had to have IVs administered every six hours around the clock through a pic line, while my foot was attached to a wound vac machine. I was utterly dependent upon Becky for my life.

All of a sudden, Becky found herself taking care of two individuals with special needs. She was already laying down her life daily to care for our son with cerebral palsy and autism. His profound special needs required her constant care and attention.

But now she had a husband with special needs who was temporarily, but completely, dependent on her for his every need as well. I was totally helpless and needed her for everything.

One day, I requested a peanut butter sandwich for lunch. Now Becky, trying to care for both of us at the same time, quickly put a dollop of peanut butter between two pieces of bread and slid it across the table.

I gazed at the sandwich for a moment. Then I made an elaborate drawn-out satirical production of separating the two pieces of bread as if I were searching fruitlessly for the peanut butter.

Waving the sandwich at her, I sarcastically said to the woman who was providing life to me, "You call this a peanut butter sandwich? This is what you gave me?"

I'll pause here while every woman reading this mutters under your breath and silently thinks, "She should have killed him right there."

Through clenched teeth, a tear running down her cheek, Becky quietly said, "Don't wave that peanut butter sandwich at me after all I'm doing for you."

At that very moment, the Spirit of God chimed in as well.

"You know, Jeff, you do the same thing to me. In a sense, you're always waving your peanut butter sandwiches at me."

Convicted, I realized just how petty and ungrateful I had been to God as well.

God has graced me with the strength to persevere and endure as a special-needs parent. God had brought me back from death and given me a second chance at life to live for him instead of me. God has taught me the essence of unconditional love, never-ending grace, and finding joy in the simple things.

He has taught me that everyone is wonderfully made, created for a plan and a purpose, and destined to glorify him. He has provided our every need and has never left my side or abandoned me on this journey.

He gives me life. He inspires and teaches me though my son, and he has made me a better person through my experiences raising a son with special needs.

And though he has chosen not to heal my son this side of heaven, he has used my son to heal me of many things I had in my life.

Like pride, selfishness, greed and arrogance, to name a few.

And yet how many times have I waved my symbolic peanut butter sandwich at God so to speak, and complained or been ungrateful over something trivial or petty in the larger scheme of life?

How many times have I let my circumstances steal my joy because I put my hope in the things of this world instead of in my trust in him? How many times have I let my every day circumstances cause anger, bitterness, despair, and frustration? How many times have I vented at God because my daily provision "didn't cover the crusts?"

He stepped out of heaven, transcended time and space, came into my world and died … because he wanted me. He came to earth looking for me because he knew I couldn't live without him.

How many times have I waved my sandwich of ingratitude, selfishness, and ungratefulness at God?

God, I'm sorry for all those peanut butter sandwiches I waved at you.

No more peanut butter sandwiches!

With his limitations due to his special needs, my son Jon Alex has a fairly predictable routine and structured day. In fact, he can go days following the same schedule and pattern with little variation.

He has no choice in the matter really. It is simply a matter of what he can and what he cannot do. His autism mandates structure and routine. His physical limitations cannot be ignored either.

I, on the other hand, am not wired that way. I need variety. I need to have different experiences each day. I have always said that I am at my best when my life is right on the edge, threatening to spin into chaos.

But I have never seen anyone in my life smile as much as my son. He constantly has a little grin on his face. In this world, he shouldn't have much to smile about at all.

Yet he is the picture of absolute joy in seemingly all things. Joy in the little things. Joy in a few things. Joy in all things.

Everyone who encounters him throughout the day comments on how he brightens his or her day. Time after time we hear about how he lifted someone's spirits or lightened their mood just by his presence.

Those made me think about myself. How many people would say the same thing about me?

Sometimes I get so wrapped up in my world and all that I have going on that I literally forget about the people around me. If I'm open and transparent, I probably go days sometimes without bringing a smile to anyone's face, much less brightening his or her day.

My wife says sometimes I look like I'm scowling even when I'm just sitting there minding my own business.

Why is it that my son can be so happy all the time when we sometimes struggle through our days?

The reason is because Jon Alex doesn't live in this world. Jon Alex's spirit is pure and untouched. His soul sings. In his world, his father loves him unconditionally, and will provide his every need.

There's a lesson there for the rest of us. When we realize that our Father loves us unconditionally and provides our every need, our joy should spill over and out. Others will see our joy, admire our faith, and we will brighten the day of everyone around us.

Think of how awesome it would be if you had the reputation of being the one who always brightened everyone else's day.

"Be thankful in all circumstances, for this is God's will for you who belong to Christ Jesus." (1 Thessalonians 5:18)

Those of you raising a child with special needs know how truly hard this is sometimes. We all have days when we want to crawl over to the Dark Side and linger for a while.

There are days I just don't feel thankful. There are days I get envious and jealous or frustrated and my attitude quickly changes colors.

My poor attitude and lack of gratitude make it tough to find something for which I'm thankful that day.

But scripture says I am to choose joy. The scriptures say it is God's will for me to remain joyful. So in order to do that, I have to change my perspective.

I have to take the same circumstances, the same situation, the same issues and look at them differently in order to choose thankfulness. It's my choice. It's not about changing my lot in life or my circumstances. It's about how I respond to my lot or circumstances.

So as a dad of a son who is nonverbal, non-mobile, and cognitively challenged, what do I have to be thankful about in my life?

I am thankful for a son who has been protected from the impurities and imperfections of this world. I am thankful for a son who I will get to be around every day for the rest of our lives. I am thankful for a son who, even at sixteen years old, hugs my neck. I am thankful for a son who taught me unconditional love. I am thankful for a son who has taught me complete dependency on God for my every need.

I am thankful for a son who has taught me to find joy in the simple things and contentment with just a few things. I am thankful for a son that God has used to help me find my purpose in life. I am thankful for a son who seems to bring out the best in everyone he encounters.

I am thankful for a son who always has a smile on his face regardless of his circumstances. I am thankful for a son who focuses on what he can do, not on what he can't do. I am thankful for a son who treasures his mother. I am thankful for a son whose name is written in the Book of Life with a permanent marker.

I am thankful that God has given my son a plan, purpose, and destiny for his life before he was ever born. Yes it would be easy to come up with a list of things for which I am not thankful. In fact, it would be very easy. After all, it's my choice.

And it's yours as well.

Choose joy. Choose thankfulness. Count it all joy, my friends.

One night, Becky and I went to a fund-raiser banquet for another local nonprofit ministry we support. So we had to arrange for a sitter for Jon Alex.

With his profound special needs, we really just have one sitter for him. She has been with us for years and has a very special bond with our son, and we trust her completely.

When we returned home after the event, she informed us Jon Alex was asleep in his room, all tucked in for the night. But when Becky slipped into his room to check on him, he was sitting up in his bed awake and watching the door! Being nonverbal, he couldn't speak up to let us know, but there he sat just waiting for us to come home and say good night.

We said good night to him and then we prayed softly over him, covered him up, and he drifted off to sleep.

This happens every time we go away for the evening. He will just sit in his bed waiting for us to return. He will not go to sleep until we have come in, spoken to him, and assured him that we are home.

He yearns for that last conversation before he can rest for the night. Sometimes he gives up if it's really late and he can't keep his eyes open. But the minute he hears us come into the house, he pops right up eagerly and expectantly.

Because to Jon Alex, we are his everything.

I was thinking about that last night and it made me wonder. *Does God sit there at night eagerly desiring to have a conversation with me before I retire for the evening?*

I bet he desires to have a conversation (prayer) with me every night. And how often do I disappoint him by not doing so because I'm tired, or busy, or have other things on my mind?

I started thinking how my son would feel if he had waited up hours just to hear from me before bed, and I let him down. What would he feel and think if I just ignored him, and went on as if he weren't there?

How disappointed he would feel.

I bet God is just like that. I bet he anxiously craves that last moment of my attention at night just like my son. He wants to be the first thing on our mind in the morning, and our last thoughts of the night.

Because God is our everything.

There are a lot of special-needs parents whose struggles challenge them to come up with any sort of list of items for which they are thankful. Deep down in our secret place, choosing to be in an attitude of gratefulness can be a challenge.

The Dark Side beckons, teases, and whispers alluringly into our ears. And this time of year when the days are short and the nights are long, it's so easy to climb into the pit, curl up, and never want to leave.

So I have to make the conscious choice to choose joy and thankfulness. I'm making the choice to be thankful for you today! I am thankful for every mom and dad of a child with special needs who stuck it out despite the odds and are raising their child together.

I am thankful for all the dads who choose to be involved and engaged—and who refuse to be a vacant dad. I'm thankful for every single parent out there raising a child with special needs alone and doing whatever it takes to find the time and resources to do so.

I'm thankful for all the bleary-eyed, sleep-deprived moms and dads who are dying daily to self and laying down their lives for their children. I'm thankful for the parents working multiple jobs to pay for therapies, medical bills, and the day-to-day expenses of having a child with special needs.

I'm thankful for every mom who, through a muffled pillow, cries herself to sleep at night so her kids won't hear her, and then gets up in the morning to boldly face the world. I'm thankful for every parent who chooses to believe his or her child is wonderfully made, created for a plan and a purpose, and destined to glorify God.

I'm thankful for every special-needs family who says, "This is our normal, and this is just how we roll!" I'm thankful that God chose us and then he called us to be parents of a child with special needs.

I'm thankful for every child with special needs who teaches us the essence of grace and unconditional love. They reveal to us the very nature of God himself. As a result, I see how amazingly gifted these individuals truly are and how we are the blessed ones just to be around them. The individuals I am privileged to be around are some of the most loving and expressive people I know.

They do not hide behind plastic faces or guard their hearts and innermost feelings. They express themselves so openly and expressively. They are not afraid to show their true, honest feelings. They make no distinctions between people like the rest of us tend to do.

Love is something to be displayed, celebrated, and demonstrated. They accept everyone on an equal footing, and make no exceptions for grace just because someone is different.

I have learned from those I know with special needs how to find the beauty in everything. They have taught me to not be in such a rush that I miss out the simplest blessings of God's creation, but to stop and notice the beauty of the world around me.

Want to understand the essence of God's unconditional love? Hang around someone with special needs. Want to learn to love as God intended? Hang around someone with special needs. Want to have your socks blessed off? Hang around folks with special needs.

I love what a friend of mine Steve says about his two chosen daughters with Down syndrome, "My girls with Down syndrome may be mentally disabled, but their hearts are not. They are so unpretentious and love others genuinely and unconditionally."

I'm thankful God does not make us walk down this path alone, but instead goes before us, alongside us, and behind us. I'm thankful God will never leave us, abandon us, or stop loving us.

I'm thankful for that coming day when he will wipe away all tears and sorrow. There will be no more death or pain, for he will make all things new.

I'm thankful that autism, cerebral palsy, Downs, seizures, and every other special needs will cease to exist in one glorious moment.

I'm thankful that I get to live in the same house as Wonder Woman and Superman.

Chapter 8
LIKE FATHER, LIKE SON

I should have seen it coming because it tends to affect me like this every year. One Friday morning on the way to work, I was listening to my favorite sports talk radio station. They were having callers call in to talk about their favorite sports memories involving their own dads. It was a Father's Day tribute show to dads.

I actually grew up with an awesome dad. Some of my favorite childhood memories involve sports and my dad.

He coached my little league baseball team. He put a basketball hoop on a telephone pole and managed to find time to play with me every day. He was a high school basketball coach and, from the age of two and up, I followed him around the gym all the time.

He coached my high school basketball teams. I got to play on the team that won his 500th game as a coach. We have conflicting memories of that night. I remember having the game-winning assist. He remembers a controversial referee's call on me that almost cost us the game. I like my recollection better.

Some of my favorite times involved the two of us going to University of Tennessee football games together. We had our standard things we did on every trip and I have a boatload of great memories. It's a tradition we've continued until a few years ago when I had to stop attending due to my son's issues.

So why do I get in a funk every year?

Every year at this time, I replay those memories in my head and I get a little melancholy and a little sad. With my son's developmental disabilities and special needs, he and I aren't able to continue those traditions.

We won't play catch in the backyard either. We won't build a tree house together. We won't watch a ballgame, ride bikes, or do any of the other typical activities dads do with their sons.

We don't go to Tennessee football games together. We can't play basketball in the driveway together. Those opportunities, like so many others I once dreamed of, aren't going to happen.

So I can't seem to help but get a little sad at the thought. But again, I have a choice in my perspective. I can still choose to find joy. With so many limits on what he can actually do, one of my son's favorite activities is swinging on his therapy platform swing. We have a therapy platform swing mounted from the ceiling in Jon Alex's room, and he loves swinging in it a couple of times a day.

One Saturday morning, in the middle of my latest pity party, I went into his room and swung him for the longest time. I made racecar sounds, plane noises, and whatever sound effects I could make to get him to giggle and smile.

Jon Alex can't talk. Never has. So I did the talking. I just talked to him, interspersing my sound effects and goofy noises.

He couldn't speak but he communicated back to me in his own way. He loved our time together and showed me at the end by hugging my neck and flashing me his big toothy grin.

And then he leaned over and kissed me on the cheek.

I'm pausing here to wipe the tears off my keyboard because I cry every time I think about it.

It wasn't what we did, or what we couldn't do together. We had just spent time together. That was all that mattered. What mattered was that we were together and I was giving him my undivided attention. That's when God spoke to me, reminding me that it's not what I do for him either. He just wants me to spend some time with him, Father to son.

And that's what I should do when I let my emotions affect me like that. I should spend some time with his Son. I'll do the talking just like with Jon Alex, but he will find a way to communicate with me in his unique ways.

And I'll leave knowing he loves me and that our time together was significant.

There was one time I could tell that Jon Alex just wasn't himself. Because he is nonverbal and can't talk, he couldn't tell me what was wrong. But I knew something wasn't right.

In the evening, he began to get a little fussy and slightly agitated. Stomachache? Overly tired? Overly stimulated? He couldn't tell me.

Before bed, I gave him a warm bath. Words can not explain how much he loves to be sung to while he is in the bathtub. Actually, he loves to be sung to anytime. He's always loved it when we sing to him and it often has a calming power when nothing else works.

So we put his pajamas on him and I carried him into his bed. He still just couldn't settle down. Something was bothering him and he couldn't find peace. I was wrecked because I wanted to help and he could not communicate to me what was going on that distressed him.

I wrapped my arms around him and I began whispering in his ears. I told him how much I loved him and how special he is to me just the way he is simply because he is my son. I told him how proud I was of him and that I would watch over him all night. I let him know I was there to take care of him and fill his every need and he had nothing to worry or be afraid about.

Finally, I began to sing over him. Softly and gently. Then he curled up, rolled over, and fell into a deep sleep.

How many times have I lain there at night all messed up? Something not right in my world, something that I will wrestle with and battle all night never finding peace, while God watches. God desires with all of heaven for me to just desire to talk to him as well. He wants to tell me he loves me unconditionally and that he will supply my every need. He wants to assure me that he can take away my fears, and will sit with me all night if I need him. And yet I'm too worked up or tired to approach him.

If only I'd ask. If only I'd stop and let him whisper in my ear reminding me of who I am in him.

He'll sing over me, too. And you. Did you know that?

Sing Daddy....

"The Lord your God is in your midst, a mighty one who will save; he will rejoice over you with gladness; he will quiet you; he will exult over you with loud singing." (Zephaniah 3:17, ESV)

Another time when he was sick, we spent the weekend unexpectedly with Jon Alex at Vanderbilt Children's Hospital. His flu got so bad it left him severely dehydrated. He had been drinking less and less until he just quit drinking at all. Saturday morning at a convenient health clinic, we were advised to take him to the emergency room for fluids.

We drove to Nashville and took Jon Alex to the emergency room at Vanderbilt Children's Hospital.

We were admitted overnight while they pumped bag after bag of fluids into Jon Alex to combat the dehydration. Becky and I both stayed in his room overnight and took turns sitting by his bedside. So the three of us braced for a long night.

Around 1:20 AM during one of my shifts, I found myself wishing and willing under my breath for him to drink. As I did so, the Lord began to speak to me in my spirit, and in doing so, gave me fresh perspective. He began to teach me in my spirit in response to what I was I whispering to Jon Alex.

"If I could just get him to drink so this would never happen again." *If you would drink from me, you would never thirst again either.*

"If he would just listen to me and trust me his father." *If you would just listen to me and trust me your Father.*

"If he would just put his faith in me to help him, he would relax and be able to rest." *If you would just come to me when you are weary and burdened, I would give you rest too.*

"I wish you could speak to me and tell me what's wrong so I could help, son." *I wish you would just speak to me when something is wrong, I could help you, too, son.*

"Son, we will go through this together. I won't leave your side." *Ditto.*

"I will stay up all night to take care of you. Nothing will separate us." *I never sleep or slumber as I watch over you in the night. And nothing can separate you from my love either.*

There was another time he felt so poorly that he could barely sit up. So Becky held him gently and whispered reassurances that it was going to be all right.

His eyes went wide as he threw up what little food he had eaten in the past twenty-four hours. So she cleaned him up and changed his pajamas.

His skin was warm to the touch because of a low-grade fever. So every few minutes, she checked his temperature to make sure it didn't climb higher.

He can't get to his bed on his own or even climb under the covers because of his special needs. So she assisted him the whole way, placed him in bed, and checked on him all through the night to make sure he stayed covered.

He was sick and feeling miserable. So she stayed by his side attending to his every need. He was up a lot at night and could not cry out if he needed her. So she stayed up with him and was there in case he did need her.

His body ached from the sickness. So she rubbed his back and neck with a soothing touch. He is pretty helpless when he gets sick. So she lays down her life to help him get better. She watched all night despite the fact that she was sick as well. That didn't matter to her. Her son with special needs needed her. So she fought through her own aches and illness so she could fight for him.

She doesn't say anything. He can't say anything.

But he knows.

And so he reached up his widespread arms and hugged her neck. And with a big toothy grin, he kissed her cheek.

Because he knew he needs her. And now she knew she needs him.

And so for one moment, I got a glimpse of the glory of the Lord. And watching them both, I realized the gift that I have received. Such extravagant beauty displayed through sacrificial service. Another storm weathered together.

One time as we turned down the road that leads into our neighborhood, the weather instantly went from bright and sunny into full-blown, wind-whipped pounding rain.

No warning. No subtle transition. No gradual change. In an instant, the storm hit with fury. But even in the storm, I could see pockets still of sunshine and blue sky. As we drove down the road leading into our neighborhood, both the power of an isolated storm and slivers of the sun surrounded us.

Suddenly right in front of us was the most vivid rainbow I've ever seen. Most of the time I've only seen partial rainbows, but this one seemed to have a definitive beginning and ending right in front of us.

Like it was just for us.

It reminded me of several years ago when we were doing a lot of testing trying to get a diagnosis of Jon Alex's special needs. We had been to Vanderbilt in Nashville for an appointment. The doctor had informed us she wanted to do an MRI looking for a possible brain tumor.

On the ninety-minute drive back to Cookeville, I couldn't speak. The emotional storm clouds rolled in and my world got dark. My thoughts and emotions swirled in my head and I couldn't get my lips to stop quivering or my tears to stop flowing.

Outside the car, a real storm rolled in and we drove home in the pounding rain. I was praying, reciting scriptures, and reminding myself that God is with us even in the storms. Suddenly, the weather had changed and, just outside my car window, a rainbow unfurled from heaven.

I knew that one was for us. It was God reminding us that he never said in this life that we wouldn't have trouble, pain, or suffering. In fact, he assured us in his word that we would have trouble and hardship. But he did promise never to leave us or forsake us. He had made a covenant.

Time after time in my life now, even in the midst of the biggest storms of raising our child, we have caught little glimmers of God's presence. Just like rainbows in a storm, God has sent us reminders of his faithfulness, protection, provision, and goodness—even in the middle of the biggest trials and struggles.

> *"When you pass through the waters, I will be with you; and through the rivers, they shall not overwhelm you; when you walk through fire you shall not be burned, and the flame shall not consume you."* (Isaiah 43:2, ESV)

I often wonder how much I would notice or even appreciate those nuggets of God's presence in my life if I didn't have to persevere through storms.

God has taught me so much by my surrendering my circumstances to him and asking him to use them-far more than I could ever learn by him simply removing the trials out of my life altogether.

God will do amazing and incredible things in our lives and walk with him if we yield our circumstances, asking him to use them instead of asking him to remove them.

I always struggle a little on Father's Day.

As the dad of a child with profound special needs, my day will be anything but that of a typical dad, or a typical Father's Day.

My son is nonverbal and so, for the sixteenth consecutive year, he won't wish me Happy Father's Day.

My son has limited motor skills, so there will be no handmade Happy Father's Day card for me.

No breakfast in bed. No handmade gifts or presents. No socks or ties. No cheesy after-shave.

No going anywhere special for the day as dad and son. No awesome planned activities just for a dad and his son.

Truthfully, my son won't even know that it is Father's Day or what that even means.

But there are some things he will notice and that will resonate with him.

When he gets up, he will find that his dad is still there. Not just there, but involved and engaged with him.

He knows he will get plenty to eat, have clothes on his back, and his every need will be attended to and provided for by his dad. He knows he can feel safe and secure, loved unconditionally and found perfect just the way he is by his dad.

He knows that before the day is over, his dad will speak blessings and prayers over him. He knows that his dad will affirm him with words of life and encouragement.

He will know how proud his dad is that he is his son.

I will be a better dad today because of him. I will be a better man today because of him. I will be a better follower of Christ today because of him.

And at the end of Father's Day, as we do every day, we will go to his room where he has a giant platform swing.

For forty-five minutes or however long he wants, I will push him in that swing. I will sing songs over him the whole time. I will juxtapose blessings and prayers over him. Nothing will be allowed to interrupt our time together.

At some point when he is ready to stop, he will make eye contact with me. That's pretty difficult for a severely autistic child. He will flash me this open-mouthed grin, and throw his arms up to hug me.

As I hold him close on his unstable legs and twisted feet, he will hug me tight, tap on my shoulders, and kiss my cheek.

No, we won't do anything special or even typical for Father's Day.

Then again, I am truly blessed though. For me, every day is Father's Day.

Neither one of us needs a card to prove it.

We are in a season right now that seems exceedingly long and stressful for me. We have so many different projects at different levels that require my attention and focus.

So as I drove home one night, I could not get my mind to slip out of work mode. All these thoughts were jockeying for position in my head. I just felt overwhelmed, and slightly out-of-control.

You've been there, haven't you? You feel exhausted and weary, but unable to relax.

Just the toll of being a parent of a child with special needs is by itself grueling, tiring, and frustratingly difficult.

You feel like your whole day is just reactive. I describe it as being the ball inside an old-fashioned pinball machine. You just bounce from one post or barrier to the next with little time to plan or think. You just roll through the day bracing for impact.

Our son with cerebral palsy and autism definitely makes our life interesting. In the evenings, to help my wife, I handle feeding Jon Alex his supper, and then we are off to swing in his platform swing in his bedroom.

It's dad's time. We swing, I sing. Jon Alex is nonverbal. Doesn't matter what I sing, he just craves that time and listening to me. On a typical night, I'll sing a few children's classics, some vintage U2 and other 1980s hits, a couple of church songs, and several made-up goofy songs of ours.

It's not what we do together as a dad. It's that I intentionally set aside a time where I am conveying that nothing else in the world matters right now but giving him my undivided attention, my whole heart, and my sole focus. Check your smartphone at the door.

My wife can't stand to listen to the singing because I never remember the actual lyrics and more or less make it up as I go.

One night, Jon Alex didn't want to swing. He hadn't slept that week much at all and it finally had caught up with him. He just wanted to go straight to "night-night" after supper. For the rest of the evening, I was restless, agitated, and just out-of-sorts.

All of a sudden, I realized why. In the beginning, that swing time was supposed to be part of Jon Alex's therapy. But now I realized it had instead become *my* therapy. That was *my* sanctuary.

This was where my mind slipped out of work mode. This was where I forgot all about my cares and concerns and focused on what really mattered. This is where I feel closest to God and his purpose for my life. I have come to crave and need those moments with him and that bedroom swing far more than Jon Alex does. I had missed my therapy.

Everyone needs to find his or her sanctuary. People try to find their sanctuary in many different forms. Some find it in television, books, comfort food, money, jobs, social media, pills, hobbies, or the Internet. Then they wonder why they feel so empty and so far from the presence of God.

I have found my sanctuary, my place where God hangs out and restores my soul. I have found my place where God renews my mind and reminds me of my purpose.

Turns out it was just down the hall.

Sometimes when I'm in a reflective or pensive mood, I just go to Jon Alex's room and sit for a few minutes. I can just sense God's Spirit there and it brings me peace.

I fell in love with the game of basketball when I was barely old enough to hold the ball between my hands. I carried that old, worn leather ball around with me everywhere I went.

Everyone in our small rural town in Tennessee knew my father simply as Coach. He spent decades coaching hundreds of boys and girls in basketball for our town's only high school.

My dad had been a star player in high school himself and, more than anything, I wanted to be like my dad. There is something inside every little boy who measures himself by his dad's achievements, and I wanted to follow in his footsteps.

One of the most joyous and yet challenging seasons of our life was when I played for him and he coached me in high school. I proudly wore number 22 and I had almost every characteristic you could want in a star player. I had passion, energy, devotion, and ball smarts. I had an uncanny ability to manage the game. I loved the game, and I had terrific leadership skills.

There was only one thing I lacked to make my game complete.

Talent.

When the game was on the line and you needed someone you could count on to make the game-winning shot, well, let's just say you hoped I stayed out of the way.

My dad had never pushed me to play basketball and he had never imposed his love for the game on me. It just came naturally out of being his son. But his love for me was never predicated or dependent upon how well I played the game that he had excelled at personally. He loved me because I was his son; it had nothing to do with my basketball ability.

We still live in that same town today. And now my own son is a freshman at that same Cookeville High School.

One morning, my wife was dressing him for school. His special education class was going on a field trip to the Special Olympics for volleyball. Even though he physically cannot participate, he enjoys riding on the bus and hanging out with his class. As she pulled his uniform shirt over his head, I was startled to see he had randomly been assigned my old number 22. I think God was in that moment, as if he did that just for me.

When we first learned we were going to have a boy, I daydreamed and fantasized constantly about someday teaching my own son the game of basketball. I would plan out what skills I would teach him first, and how I would methodically mold him into the superstar I never was. I had dreamed that he would be the next Davidson to wear number 22. Now here was my son wearing a uniform with my old number on it.

My dream was to coach my son just as my dad had coached me. I had even purchased a full-sized basketball goal and had it in the driveway ready and waiting before he was born.

But autism and cerebral palsy had other plans. With his special needs, I quickly realized those dreams would have to die. There would not be three generations of Davidsons playing basketball in the driveway together.

At first, it was difficult coming to terms with laying down those dreams. Like any special-needs dad, it's hard emotionally to reach the point where you realize the dreams, goals, and plans you had for your child aren't going to happen the way you hoped. But whose dream was it anyway? It wasn't God's dream.

This is where the choice happens for dads. You can choose to spend the rest of your life wallowing in the "Why" and grieving the dead dreams. Most men choose this route. At the end of their journey, they find they have been following a dead-end street that goes nowhere.

Or you can go down the road marked "How." How are we going to rise above this situation and still find the glory and purpose that God has in this? How can we use this different dream to still find fulfillment and joy?

My son will never do anything that makes me love him anymore than I already do. I love him because he is my son.

Period.

I made him. I created him. He was formed in my image. And for that, I love him unconditionally. Nothing he can ever do will make me love him any more than I already love him. If all he ever does in life is just be my son, that is enough. My love for him is unconditional.

I got that from my dad. Not just the one here on earth, but the One who made all of us as well.

Why do we think we have to do something to earn God's love or make him love us more than he does? He made you, he created you in his image, and he knit you together in your mother's womb.

Don't let anyone try to lie to you, try to deceive you, or try to persuade you otherwise. Nothing you ever do will make God love you more than he already does now. He loves you because you are his son or his daughter.

Period.

God is not punishing you. God has not abandoned you. God has not forgotten you. God's love for you is everlasting, never failing, and never ending. Doesn't matter whether you can hit a jump shot or not!

My dad is a man of very few words. Growing up, he never really vocalized love for his kids, but he left no doubt where he stood by his actions, his interactions, and his engaging with us. He always called me "Bud." No wonder I'm always calling my own son "Buddy."

Somewhere deep inside of every little boy is the burning desire to earn his father's love and respect. It's not something discussed or even admitted to most of the time, as most males aren't comfortable expressing their emotions that way.

It's why little boys are always begging for their dads to watch them do something, or attempting a great feat like jumping a ditch on their bike, throwing a football, or leaping out of a swing. Some say they are just crying out for attention when what they are really crying out for is approval.

That feeling never goes away by the way. No matter how old we get as men, deep down, we still want our father's approval and respect. It's a way we measure whether we have become a man in our own right.

This week, my wife Becky and I were being interviewed and the question was asked, "What do you enjoy the most about your son Jon Alex?"

I thought for a minute and then I replied, "What I enjoy the most is the simple fact that he is my son. There is nothing he can do to make me love him more. He is the best son I could ask for simply because he is my son."

I tell Jon Alex that every night. I want it to be one of the last things he hears before he goes to sleep.

I always conclude it by saying, "You are the best son in the whole wide world and I wouldn't want any other boy but you, because God made you for me, and God made me for you."

The words that you speak over your child or about your child have the power of life and death. I am constantly, with every opportunity I have, speaking positive words of affirmation and life over my son. I am constantly telling him how proud I am to be his dad and how honored I am that God chose him to be my son.

I thought of this the other day when I met a stranger. He was shuffling around in the parking lot as I pulled into the office early one morning.

Before I had even got out of the car, he had wandered over and was standing by my car, obviously waiting for me to get out.

I nodded to him and said hello as I headed to our office's front door. He followed me curiously and noticed our name on the door. He asked me "What is Rising Above Ministries?"

I invited him to join me inside where he explained he was waiting for the office next door to open for business. I briefly described who we are and what we do for the special-needs community. I was in a hurry to get started on my tasks for the day, but he was a talkative older man, and so I listened politely.

Over the next five or ten minutes as we talked, he mentioned that he had an adult son with special needs himself.

Only he didn't use the words "special needs."

He called his own son retarded. In fact, he used the word retarded five to six times in the brief few moments he was in my office. Over and over, the word rolled off his tongue.

My blood pressure went up twenty points every time the word came out of his mouth. The word is offensive and appalling to me and to the special-needs community. He even shared with me a story where his own son was struggling to do a task, and he told his son to give up, saying, "You can't do it because you're retarded."

Just as I was beginning to consider a Jedi mind trick to try to blow him up right in front of me, I sensed the Holy Spirit calming me down.

He was an older man, and, in his generation, the word was commonly used and socially acceptable those many years ago. For those reasons, I decided this time I would give grace.

But all week long now, I can't stop thinking about that poor son. Having your own dad tell you to give up because you are retarded. Telling you that you cannot do something because "you're retarded."

The words you speak over your child or about your child have the power of life and death. I am constantly, with every opportunity I have, speaking positive words of affirmation and life over my son. I am always telling him how proud I am to be his dad and how honored I am that God chose him to be my son.

And we have a rule to never speak negatively about him to others either. I constantly tell him how much I love him the way he is and I wouldn't wish for any other boy but him.

There's an interesting passage in scripture. In the Book of Matthew chapter 21, verses 18-20, Jesus has an unusual encounter with a fig tree.

"In the morning, as Jesus was returning to Jerusalem, he was hungry, and he noticed a fig tree beside the road. He went over to see if there were any figs, but there were only leaves. Then he said to it, 'May you never bear fruit again!' And immediately the fig tree withered up. The disciples were

amazed when they saw this and asked, 'How did the fig tree wither so quickly?'" (Matthew 21:18-20)

Jesus spoke death over the fig tree and it never bore fruit again. The tree simply withered and died. His words had the power of life and death.

So do your words.

Your child with special needs is your fig tree. Every time you pass by or encounter your child, you need to speak words of life, love, and affirmation over your child or children.

Your spouse is a fig tree. Every time you pass by your spouse is an opportunity to speak life into your spouse as well. Water the trees in your life. Nourish your trees in your life. Speak life over your trees.

Your words will be the difference between life and death.

Speak words of life and affirmation over your children.

Your child was fearfully and wonderfully made in God's own image. The writer of James says this about our tongues. *"Sometimes it praises our Lord and Father, and sometimes it curses those who have been made in the image of God. And so blessing and cursing come pouring out of the same mouth. Surely, my brothers and sisters, this is not right! Does a spring of water bubble out with both fresh water and bitter water?"* (James 3:9-11)

How can the same mouth that praises God also curse things created in God's own image?

I am a man of so many faults and imperfections who fails daily and is totally dependent on the grace of his God. But my son will never be in doubt of my love and belief in him just the way he is. Maybe that's why I am so passionate about fighting the vacant dad epidemic we have in the special-needs community.

I was blessed with a dad who always encouraged me, often even without words. There is an old poem about choosing "the road less traveled." Well, I have veered down an even more off the beaten path road in my life.

When I gave up a full college scholarship to transfer to another university and switch majors, a lot of people thought I was crazy. My dad never said a negative word, just that he supported me.

When I turned forty, I walked away from the corporate life, the dream home, and the six-digit income. We sold most everything we owned, took an eighty percent pay cut, and moved into the country because I felt a calling to start a special-needs ministry. My dad encouraged and supported me. At the time, everyone thought we were nuts. Once again, my dad never said a negative word, just that he believed in me.

When I turned forty-two, I had some serious health issues and almost died on a hospital table. I spent months in a wheelchair recuperating afterwards. My dad hardly ever left my side.

This weekend, we attended the memorial service for the dad of my friend Steve. Steve is a pastor friend of mine, and also the father of two children with special needs himself.

Steve was sharing some of his favorite stories about his dad throughout the service. His love, respect, and admiration for his late father was so evident as he eulogized his dad with tears streaming down his face and his voice soft and tender. At the end of his moving remarks, though, he said something that made me look up and take note.

Steve said his father didn't leave a lavish estate, a big inheritance, or a nice car. The legacy he left that mattered the most to Steve was that his father had been proud of him. He said knowing how great a man his dad was, and knowing that his dad was proud of him as his son, was something to be treasured and would never be forgotten.

There is something inside of a man that always wants his dad to be proud of him. It's with us from the moment we are born; we want our dads to be proud of the men we become, and to know how much they value us as their sons.

A few months ago during a particularly rough and testing season for us as a special-needs family, I took a quick walk on the Dark Side and threw myself a pity party. I questioned my calling, my purpose, and whether I was making a difference.

My dad, who is not an expressive man at all with his emotions, sent me a card out of the blue telling me how proud he was that I had chosen this path for my life, and that he could not be more pleased that I was his son.

I sat in my office and openly wept that afternoon. I still keep the card in my right hand desk drawer. That card is priceless to me. It's the best gift he has ever given me. That's why I keep it in the front drawer of my desk.

Because what he was really saying is "I love you because you are my son."

Period.

Nothing else matters. I have his respect and validation just by virtue of being his son.

I get asked all the times by parents of children with special needs how to get dads more involved and engaged. Here's an easy way, Dads.

Dads, your words contain the power of life and death.

Parents, you have got to be speaking words of life over your kids every day. Your kids will believe whatever you say about them. Your child will become whatever he or she believes. And what they believe about themselves will be determined by what you speak over them. They will become whatever the voices they hear say about them. So make a point, every day, to speak positively and affirm your child.

At sixteen my son is nonverbal. Barring a miracle, he won't be able to stand up at my funeral and tell the world how proud I was of him. But rest assured, he knows it. And that's all that matters. We can talk about it in heaven someday.

I love my son just the way he is because my dad loves me just the way I am. Not because of anything I have done, or am doing, or will ever do. I learned unconditional love for my son because my dad loves me unconditionally.

My friends, this is the essence of how God loves us. We don't earn it, we don't do anything to deserve it—he just lavishes it on us simply because we are his children.

There is nothing we can do that will earn us more love from him or make him love us more. He loves us simply because we are his children.

I am still amazed and astonished to realize that as much as I love Jon Alex, God loves him even more than I do. I cannot imagine it possible to love my son more than I do, but God does.

So that's how I choose to love. Like father, like son.

Chapter 9
LESSONS FROM THE NEW NORMAL

We live just outside of town and when it storms, we frequently lose our electricity temporarily. When it happens at night, we are surrounded by total blackness because of our location.

Whenever we get a storm at night with lots of thunder and lightning, I can't sleep. I will lie awake just waiting for the storm to pass. Often, this is when the storm will knock the power off for a few minutes.

Our son as I've mentioned is completely nonverbal. He also can't get up and walk on his own either. So if the storms and darkness scare him, he really has no way to tell us. He can't tell us what he is feeling or if he is afraid. And he can't leave his bed to find us either.

I go into his room whenever this happens. I can't really see him, so I begin to speak to him, telling him what is going on. I stretch out my arm over his bed and I put my hand where he can reach it.

Out of the darkness, I will feel his little hand reach up and hold tightly onto mine. So we just sit there in the silence, and he holds onto my hand.

It's never too dark, and the storm is never too great, if you know where your father is.

Life is just like that, too, you know. When you walk through the heavy stuff, when the storms you're facing threaten to overwhelm you, when your life is so dark you can't move—reach out to the Father and take his hand.

Because it's never too dark, and no storm is too great, if you know where to find your Father's hand.

I have to be the least musically gifted man walking the earth. I can't play any instruments and I certainly can't sing. I admire those who can, and I get envious of their abilities and gifts. My childhood past is littered with failed attempts at lessons in both guitar and piano.

The most humiliating experience was a few years ago. My son Jon Alex has always loved for us to sing over him. For the longest time, the only way I could get him to relax at night and fall asleep was to sing "Jesus Loves Me" over and over.

So I decided to take guitar lessons one more time just to learn that one song. I was told it only takes three simple chords to learn. Every Friday for several weeks, I had a local worship leader come over to the office and try to teach me that song on the guitar.

The poor guy had never had a student as bad as me. We spent months just trying to master that song. Finally, the big moment arrived. I gathered Becky and Jon Alex together in the den and performed my masterpiece!

When I was done, I looked expectantly at my wife, who said, "That was good ... what was it?" She didn't even recognize "Jesus Loves Me" when I tried to play it! I remember thinking, *It's so simple, how come I can't get it?*

I was thinking about that one weekend. I see so many people who feel abandoned, forgotten, and tossed aside. I see so many people living in fear, shame, and guilt who cannot let go of the past.

I see so many people trying to work their way into heaven. I see people crushed under the false notion that they have to do something to earn God's love and grace. I see so many people who just feel unlovable and unusable. And I scream inside, "It's so simple, why can't we learn it?"

"Jesus loves me, this I know. For the Bible tells me so." Just like the song says.

It really is that simple. If only we could grasp what it truly means. It means you can let go of the past. It means you can forgive yourself and pick yourself back up. It means your life has a purpose, a plan, and a destiny.

It means you don't have to seek approval from others or validation and self-worth based on what others think. It means you are not being punished for your past. It means you haven't been forgotten or abandoned.

It means everything. And it really is that simple. Some of us learned that song in kindergarten. If only we understood it now.

With a son in the school special education system, we have sat through dozens of meetings with teachers, therapists, and service providers over the years. I always dread the meetings and approach them with some trepidation. No one likes to hear just how far behind one's child is, especially when you hear it over and over every time.

Becky and I were talking about our most recent meeting the other day. One of his therapists was at the point of exasperation as if to say, "Nothing we've done works, I don't know what else to try or do."

As parents, we're stubborn sometimes about our children, believing deep down that they have potential and shouldn't be judged by the past or even present circumstances. We want to scream, "Don't give up! You don't know him like I do! I believe in his potential."

That explains God the Father so vividly, doesn't it? To him, your past is irrelevant, too, and certainly not indicative of your future potential or ability. He's a dad and he believes in his kids, too.

He told the prophet Jeremiah, *"I knew you before I formed you in your mother's womb. Before you were born I set you apart."* (Jeremiah 1:5)

In other words, God has a purpose and plan for every life, including yours and your child's. And nothing will stand in the way of fulfilling God's chosen destiny. Your past can't get in the way, and your previous behavior or abilities have nothing to do with God accomplishing his will for your life when you surrender it to him.

Something else I'm learning: As upset and disheartened as I get when I hear the negative aspects of what my son can't do, I'm ashamed to say I do the same thing.

We are so quick to rush judgment and to focus on the negative things in others' lives, aren't we? What if we extended grace to others as easily and quickly as we expect it for ourselves? I readily accept and receive grace a whole lot quicker and easier than I give grace to others.

Imagine the difference it would make in our lives and the lives of those around us.

Early on, I would have to politely leave the room when friends began talking about the latest milestone their child had reached. My emotions were so intensely raw and so on edge, I couldn't bear to hear them talk about little Bobby's latest accomplishment.

I really thought those feelings would go away someday. I really did. For the most part, they have gone away. For the most part, I have compartmentalized those emotions and feelings. I've put them in a quarantined section of my heart where I don't allow admittance.

But now that Jon Alex is a teenager, I find myself fighting them all over again. Every dad dreams of helping his son come of age. It's a rite of passage that goes back to the origins of man. We all dream of helping our sons transition into manhood.

Teaching them to drive a car.
Teaching them how to knot a tie.
Teaching them how to handle money.
Attempting to teach them how to interact with women
(pretending we know the answer ourselves.)
Teaching them responsibility and accountability.
Teaching them our values, our faith, and our virtues.

The one that tripped me up this week was shaving.

As my son is now sixteen, his facial hair is coming in strong. The basic formations of a little mustache already appear over his upper lip. So we bought an electric razor to use on him.

But instead of teaching him how to shave, I am coming to terms that I will be the one shaving him for the rest of my life. Every day I will shave myself, and then attempt to shave my son with special needs.

It's a bag of twisted and thorny emotions when a dad realizes he will have to shave his son for the rest of his life. And my son absolutely hates having anything near his face, certainly not touching it. This morning I was in a real funk, so I went home and went before the Lord. I didn't say anything at all, I just needed to sit in his presence and hope he would speak to me.

As I did, the Lord brought to my mind the image of Christ right before his betrayal and death. He was in the Upper Room with his disciples for the last time. What did he do? What did he need them to know the most? What was the most important lesson they had to learn?

"After that, he poured water into a basin and began to wash his disciples' feet, drying them with the towel that was wrapped around him." (John 13:5)

In that moment, God revealed to me that he has called me to lay down my life to serve my son. Shaving my son every day is a simple way of emulating Christ. That in effect, I am picking up my own towel and basin and becoming more Christlike thorough that simple act.

And every day I will have a choice. I can wallow in self-pity that I have to do this for him. Or I can be grateful that the Lord has given me a daily reminder of Christ's sacrifice and how he laid down his own life for me.

I know what I will choose.

Our church home has an annual father-son retreat they call Man Camp. Dads take their preteen and teenage sons off for the weekend together. Over the two days, they will mentor and teach them what it means to be a man.

They will have sessions on basic car repair, using power tools, firearms classes, camping, kayaking, games, and canoeing. Interspersed throughout the weekend will be talks on virtues, purity, faith, and the responsibilities of being a man.

This is something our church has done every year. Every time we have done one before, it has produced great sadness inside of me. After all, my son with profound special needs cannot participate in these types of endeavors. So we never are able to go to this type of events.

I used to get really depressed because the whole experience reminds me yet again of how different our lives are, and how limited we are in what our son can do and enjoy. My son, of course, is totally oblivious to the whole thing. I am the one with the attitude problem. So once again this year, we will not be at Man Camp, and I will not be teaching him how to be a man.

Instead, we will spend our weekend together in our customary ways. I will swing him in his platform swing over and over as it is his favorite activity. We will go for rides together in the car and let him bounce in his seat. We will sit side by side on the couch as I speak blessings over him and scratch his back.

Saturday night we will host a worship service for those with special needs. It's part of a ministry birthed out of our experiences with him. On Sunday, we will go to church and he will participate in our special-needs ministry there that was started because of him.

Then on Sunday, he will go to his papa's eightieth birthday party in Nashville where he will light up his grandfather's face and cause him to break out in song, singing over Jon Alex.

Joy can be found in the simplest of things.
Happiness and contentment can be found with just a few things.
Dying to oneself means living sacrificially for others.

It's about being together, not what you do together. There is no greater or nobler endeavor than to love unconditionally.

There is nothing Jon Alex can do to make me love him any more or any less than I do already. I love him unconditionally simply because he is my son. And if that is all he ever is in life, that's enough for me. He is my son and nothing can change my love for him.

In that respect, Jon Alex is teaching me to be more like Jesus, and to truly grasp how much God loves me just because I'm his son. So I guess you can say that Jon Alex and I are having our own Man Camp.

The only difference is that he is the teacher and I am the pupil. And he teaches me what it's really like to be a man.

I've decided there are another two types of people in the world: Those who always make sure they have gas in their car's tank, and those of us who live on the edge. My wife is among the first kind of people. When her gas gauge indicates she has about a quarter of a tank left, she immediately starts looking for a gas station to fill up her tank.

For whatever reason, I'm the opposite. I'm the guy who thinks he can still go a long way after the fuel light indictor comes on. In fact, I get a rush out of seeing just how far I can go sometimes on empty.

I know better.

After running out of gas eight times, believe me, I know better.

But I can't stop doing it. It's just a matter of time before I do it again. Eight times now in my life I have run out of gas in my car. Fortunately, the majority of the time it's been in my own neighborhood or even my own driveway. But twice this year I've run out of gas on the way to work, including once on the interstate.

I admit I can't seem to change the behavior. The fuel gauge gets under a quarter of a tank, *no problem.* Now it's under an eighth of a tank, *plenty of gas left.* The fuel light just came on, *everyone knows you can still go a good 20 miles with the light on.*

I always seem to wait until I'm completely empty before stopping to fill up my tank again. And so sometimes I just go completely dry.

There is always something to do, somewhere to go, something more urgent or important than stopping to fuel up. *I'll do it this evening. I'll do it tomorrow. I'll fill up soon, just not right now.*

I find myself doing the same thing in my spiritual life. Instead of taking time every day to fill my tank—by reading and meditating on scripture or spending extended time in prayer and reflection—I keep putting them off. I make something else a priority or a more urgent task.

I'll get to that just as soon as I....

Before long, I find my spiritual tank completely dry because I waited too long to fuel up and now it's empty. In each of our lives, we have things that fill our tanks and things that drain our tanks. Those of you raising children with special needs know the unique things that drain our tanks daily. All of us know the things we all face that can drain our tanks—jobs, careers, worrying over finances, raising children, tasks and responsibilities.

Each of us faces more than enough things every day to completely drain our tanks.

And if we don't make it a priority—the main thing, to fill our tanks every day—we'll run on empty and dry up. Fill your tank up every day. You need spiritual fuel for maximum efficiency and performance. Just like your car engine needs gas.

Take it from a guy who has sat stranded on the side of highway in a blazing sun with the smell of diesel fuel from semitrucks up his nose, wishing his priorities had been different that day. Fill up!

Do you ever have mornings where you get out of bed thinking, *My spiritual tank's empty, I just don't have anything left today.* Your own internal tank is empty and needs immediate filling.

I was like that recently. We had been running a real hard pace at our ministry getting ready for a month full of activities. And on top of that, our son was going through one of his sleepless seasons.

That weekend we had one of our special-needs worship services here in Cookeville. I sat in the back watching and waiting to deliver the message, praying for God to infuse me with energy. All of a sudden, God opened my eyes to what was going on around me. I witnessed a young man with cerebral palsy struggle to his feet and stand up when the song lyrics "I will rise" were being sung.

I watched two boys with profound special needs sitting side-by-side with t-shirts that said on the back, "I am wonderfully made and created for a plan and a purpose." Behind me, an intellectually challenged young adult belted out worship songs at the top of his lungs singing about being free. And when it came time for the children to gather around and sing a couple of children's worship songs, I watched the miraculous.

A fourteen-year-old boy with autism led the children's worship. Not just a fourteen-year-old boy, but also a boy who was practically nonverbal just three years ago. A boy who spoke his first complete sentence when he came to our special-needs Vacation Bible School and, by the end of the week, sang, "Jesus Loves Me."

Now here he was leading his friends and other children in praising God just three years later!

I couldn't understand a lot of his words or what he was singing. But he wasn't singing to me or for me. His audience was the Director of Music himself, Christ Jesus. He had an audience of one. And I guarantee Jesus understood it all, received it all, and was glorified by it all.

A new mom to our group who drove an hour to attend our gathering smiled broadly as her own son with autism danced and twirled to the music. I needed a reminder of why we do what we do that night. I needed to have my tank filled. And I needed to be reminded of how big God really is. I left with my soul singing, my tank overflowing, and my spirits renewed.

I used to think God called me to be a missionary to the special-needs community. Now I think maybe sometimes he has called them to be a missionary to me.

Most mornings start much earlier than I would have hoped. Our son's autism dictates our schedule every day. In fact, as those of you raising a child with special needs know, your whole life is pretty much dictated by that child.

Whenever Jon Alex wakes up, he doesn't have any concept of time. So whether it's 3:00 AM or 5:00 AM, he just assumes it's time to get up. Being nonverbal, he first makes his unique sounds, then he gets louder and louder until we go in to see and greet him.

He usually needs to be attended to first thing. Our entire morning routine revolves around him and attending to his needs. At breakfast, Becky prays over him and they spend time together as he eats his breakfast. This continues on as they get in the van and drive to his school.

In the evenings after work, I swing him in his platform swing. That time becomes our quiet time together. I pray over him and speak blessings and scripture over him. I always end by thanking him for being my son and remind him that God created him to be my son. I tell him that we were made for each other and I wouldn't want anyone else as my son but him.

Our evenings again revolve around him—dinnertime, bath time, story time, and bedtime. He determines when we go shopping, how we go out, where we go out, what we do and what we don't do. He is the center of our world. All of our plans revolve around him.

I stopped this morning to realize how much God wants and deserves the same from me. He should be the center of my life and world. Everything in my life should revolve around him. Every aspect of my life should be altered and affected by our relationship.

How God must crave me praying with him in the mornings and evenings. How he must want me to alter what I do and don't do because of my relationship with him. How he surely must want me to plan every aspect of my life around his presence in my life.

He wants me to acknowledge I was made for him and his love for me should compel me to want nothing more. He must yearn to speak blessings over my life when I sit, listen, and spend time with him. In so many ways, I am his son with special needs. I think that is why he is able to help me so much in this walk as a dad of a son with special needs.

I remember a time when Jon Alex went through a couple of weeks very sick. He had strep throat, pink eye, and a sinus infection simultaneously. For several days, despite medication, the little guy couldn't sleep. He couldn't breathe comfortably and was just full of congestion in his nose and throat. His eyes were all caked over.

Because of his special needs, he couldn't blow his own nose or do anything really to alleviate his symptoms on his own. So he was incapable of helping himself. Being nonverbal, he couldn't even tell us what he needed. The doctor told us he was highly contagious and warned us to try to be careful.

One night, I could hear him coughing, sneezing, and moaning as he tried to go to sleep. He would lie down but couldn't breathe as he was all stopped up. So he would sit up and moan, having not been able to sleep for several nights.

I went into his room and pulled up a chair to his bedside. Jon Alex's bed, because of his mobility issues, sits lower on the floor than a typical bed. As I sat there looking down at him in his bed, I tried softly singing to him and praying gently to him.

As I did so, he reached his arms up towards me. I froze for just a second. With my immune system, I knew that if I picked him up or got too close, I would get the same sickness he had. But what kind of dad would ignore his son's need for help? Without a second thought, I knew I had to go down in there to bring him relief.

There was no other way.

I lowered the protective bed rail, reached in, and grabbed my son. He instantly rolled into my shoulder and rested his head on my chest. I held him in my lap leaning against me, and he flashed a little smile as he drifted off to sleep.

I don't think I have ever felt the unconditional love a dad has for his child any stronger than in that moment. And yes, two days later, I developed strep throat, pink eye, and a sinus infection. But my son was much better!

In looking back a couple of weeks later, I saw that what God was doing through this experience was showing me the essence of the Gospel and why Jesus did what he did.

We were helpless and covered in our own sickness called sin. And because of our sickness, we were separated from God. God looked at our situation and knew that the only way to save us was to take on our sickness himself. So God in the form of Jesus said, "I'm going down there. It's the only way."

This journey of being a special-needs parent is so challenging and demanding. Not to mention the weariness and loneliness we sometimes feel. Have you ever had one of those days when you just feel helpless and don't know where to turn?

Next time it happens, just stretch your arms up towards the heavens and cry for help.

You may be in a mess, but God wants you to know you are his mess. And when you reach for him, he won't pause for a second to come down here for you.

He's a special-needs dad himself, you know. That's what fathers do. They clean up their children's messes.

Orville Redenbacher would have shrieked in dismay at the sight on the floor.

Pieces of popcorn littered the floor in all directions, looking like a small hailstorm had blown through the room just minutes earlier.

We had just celebrated at my son Jon Alex's sixteenth birthday party. For months, we had planned for this big day. His profound special needs severely limit him, but we wanted to celebrate and honor him in a huge way.

So the DJ played, the throngs of kids with special needs rocked out, the food was over-the-top, and the party rolled. I sat with my son, feeding him popcorn while watching kids in wheelchairs and walkers doing the limbo and forming a conga line.

Jon Alex is on a fairly restricted diet, so air-popped popcorn is one of his favorite snacks. He was snatching it out of my hand in clumps faster than I could reload. Mouthful after mouthful, one after another, he ate the popcorn.

I could tell he was really enjoying the scenes around him as he munched away. The only problem was that his limited motor skills, in conjunction with my feeding methods and his hurried approach, resulted in only about a third of the bag actually making its way into his mouth. The remainder of the bag's contents would eventually fall to the floor or on him.

So when I tell you he had six bags of popcorn at the party, it was really more like two, as four bags worth fell on the floor around us or all over him. Simply put, my son had made an absolute mess! But with his special needs, he wasn't capable of cleaning up the mess himself.

Dad had to step in.

No judgment, no harsh words, no rush to condemn. I cleaned up the mess he was in, because he couldn't do it himself. That's what dads do. We come alongside and take care of the mess. All of a sudden, I was struck by the lesson God had just showed me. God had just taught me an important lesson about grace.

Grace is God the Father doing for his children what they can't do for themselves.

Our lives are a mess sometimes, right? Doctor's appointments, therapies, medical bills, IEPs, finances, insurance battles, not to mention the everyday chaos we face.

Despite our best efforts to hold it together, despite our best efforts to manage and cope, despite our best efforts to survive- sometimes we just feel like we are wallowing in a mess and we can't get out. And like a helpless child, sometimes you just can't clean up the mess on your own.

That's what God means by grace. Surrendering your problems to him, admitting you have made a mess of things and can't do this on your own, and allowing him, like the Dad he is, to come alongside you and clean up your mess.

I am always inspired and encouraged when we have one of our Rising Above worship services for the special-needs community. Sometimes I just watch the children as they interact with each other or during children's worship, and I am amazed at how much they teach us. We always call the children down to the front of the room for a special time of children's worship. We sing fun songs with lots of movements and interactive gestures. Special buddies assist the children who need it so that everyone despite the disability gets to participate.

There was a moment once when I looked up on stage at the volunteers leading the worship time and saw a tender, beautiful scene unfold. The two volunteers who were leading had been joined on stage by two of our children with special needs.

One little boy has such a deformity in his feet that he can't wear shoes. He was dancing before the Lord while standing on the tops of his toes as they were curled and tucked in behind his feet. Beside him stood another boy who was born without the middle part of his brain.

And here they were leading all of us in worshipping God. In front of them were all these kids with disabilities and special needs dancing, singing, and in their own unique ways celebrating and praising God.

Watch these kids long enough and you begin to realize that they don't make any distinctions or notice any differences about each other. They don't define other people or label other people. They don't elevate or place one person or group over others. They don't pay attention to how they are different. They simply focus on what they have in common.

They focus on what unites them, not what divides them. In their eyes, they are all equal. They are more alike than different. As such, they encourage each other. They play together, celebrate together, and cry together. They are better together.

And I think of how much better our world would be if we were just like them.

What if we recognized that we are all broken? What if we recognized we are all wounded? What if we all focused on doing life together?

What if we learned to worship with passion and to worship uninhibited? What if we learned like them to look at what unites us? What if we learned to be better together? Sometimes I just sit back and wonder, *Who is teaching whom?*

There was a time when we were at the hospital with Jon Alex for some neurological tests. I sat beside the hospital bed anxiously waiting. How long would it take for the anesthesia to kick in? How long will the test then take? What if he has a reaction to the medicine they used to put him under?

He knew something different was happening. He was in a strange place. People were hooking him up to all kinds of electrical monitors and equipment. There were all these people he did not know in the room all dressed alike.

He looked at me as if to say, *What is going on?* As I prayed silently over him, I reached out and took his hand and squeezed it. As I did so, I looked down and was struck by the image of my son's hand in my hand, with identical identifying wristband.

The hospital had placed those wristbands on us when we arrived for the test. They were proof that he belonged to me, and that I belonged to him. They had our names on them and symbolized our relationship. If anyone had any doubt that he was my son and I was his father, all they had to do is glance at our hands.

Here I was holding my whole world by holding my son's hand. As if I were saying, *You are always in my thoughts, you are constantly present in my head. I will never leave you, abandon you, or ask you to walk through this alone because you are my son. So much so that this wristband is as if you were indelibly marked on my hand. You are mine, and I am yours.*

I am reminded of the verse by which God tells his people the same thing. He says, "*See, I have engraved you on the palms of my hands; your walls are ever before me.*"(Isaiah 49:16, ESV)

God tells his people he has written their names on his hands. In other words, he says, I have marked you as belonging to me. I never stop thinking about you; I never stop caring about you. I never stop loving you. I have marked you as mine, and nothing can ever change that. I am here, and I always will be.

Sometimes when the storms hit, it's very easy to lose sight of this.

"Where's God?"
"Has God left us?"
"Does God care?"
"Am I going to walk down this path alone?"

God wants to remind us that he has written our names on his hand. He constantly thinks about us, and would never ask us to go through this journey without his presence.

No matter how brutal the storm you are facing....
No matter how high the waves are crashing....
No matter how strong the wind is blowing....
No matter how high the waters get....
No storm is too great for you when you know where to find your father's hand.

As we travel down this path, God is always speaking, always teaching, and always revealing new lessons from our new normal.

Chapter 10
TALES FROM THE DARK SIDE

My wife and I use the phrase Dark Side to refer to that feeling of temporary grief, depression, or discouragement that we feel from time to time as parents of a child with special needs.

So many people tell you, as the parent of a child with special needs, that you just have to fully go through the grief process until you come to a place of peace.

What I have learned as the father of a child with special needs and as a special needs pastor is that you will go through that grief period over and over, several times throughout your life. Not only that, but you and your spouse will go through those stages at your own paces, meaning you aren't at the same place in your grief at the same time.

We have developed the concept of the Dark Side to give ourselves the liberty, grace, freedom, and space needed to cope and deal with periods of discouragement, sadness, grief, as we struggle down this journey. We call these periods the Dark Side.

Everyone has certain triggers that can cause a walk on the Dark Side. So here are our ground rules for surviving a walk on the Dark Side.

1) Only one of us can go there at a time. Misery loves company. When we throw a pity party, our natural tendency is to invite others to join us. To survive a walk on the Dark Side, only one person can go at a time. The other person in the relationship must stay positive and unaffected, refusing to join in the walk on the Dark Side.

2) You cannot survive staying on the Dark Side too long. We give each other a few days and that is it. If you stay there too long mentally, it will destroy you. So if one of us ventures over, the other can leave us alone initially, but eventually has to come perform search and rescue.

3) You must have a trusted friend/spouse/someone who will faithfully throw you a lifeline and come pull you out at the appropriate time without judgment, comment, or question.

4) Don't be afraid of the Dark Side. You can grow, mature, and learn from a walk on the Dark Side. Just obey the rules!

I remember when we had our annual IEP meeting for our son Jon Alex as he prepared to go to high school. This particular IEP had a little more significance than many previous ones. Jon Alex had spent the last several years in the same CDC class with the same teacher at the same school.

With his autism and cerebral palsy, the old team he had worked with had passionately poured into him and knew him so well.

With the coming school year though, he would be transitioning from his middle school to a 2,300-student high school. That meant a new teacher, a new school, and a new environment. It also meant new therapists and new assistants. So much in his little world was going to be new for him. Transitions, changes in routine, and changes in structure can be difficult on children with autism.

As we sat in the conference room for the meeting, my mind kept drifting to the fact that my son was now going to be in high school. I thought back to my own high school experiences and compared them to what my son's will be like. The experience will be so different for him.

He is nonverbal, and mobility impaired. His day will revolve around the therapeutic services he receives and discrete trials to learn new skills. The longer I thought about this transition in his life, the closer I came to flirting with the Dark Side.

For me, transitional moments seem to trigger my own walks on the Dark Side: the first time I realized I have to shave him every day for the rest of his life; when others his age began to apply for driver's license permits, and their dads were looking at cars; when football season rolls around every fall and families begin to plan family outings to watch the games in person.

Surviving the Dark Side means giving oneself permission to go there occasionally.

Surviving the Dark Side means recognizing your triggers and realizing you can only visit, not take up permanent residence!

We met his new teacher and toured his new classroom, but apprehension and nervousness still dominated our thoughts. Becky wished she had a Jon Alex app for her smartphone that she could just download for everyone who would be working with him. This one hit me hard initially. But then I relied on what I always preach to others. The Dark Side is a destination that you choose. You can't be forced to go there.

So I chose not to go to the Dark Side. I chose not to go because these things are undeniably true. He won't be going out for the football or basketball team. He won't be auditioning for the marching band. He won't be entering the science fair or qualifying for the Academic Bowl. He won't be working on the homecoming float or decorating for the prom. He won't learn to drive a car this year or get his driver's license. He won't ask any girls out on a date or attend any dances.

Cerebral palsy and autism have robbed him of all those typical high school opportunities. Being nonverbal, mobility-impaired, and cognitively impaired will dramatically rob our family of several aspects of his high school years. As I dwelled on this, I started to struggle. But then I made the choice to focus on the flip side.

These things are also true and will also be robbed of us. I'll never get a phone call that he wrecked the car while it was full of his friends. I'll never have to worry that he is trying drugs or drinking for the first time. I'll never pace the floor in the middle of the night wondering where he is, what he is doing, or when he will get home.

I'll never have to question his judgment in choosing friends or who he allows to influence him. I'll never have to worry that he is crossing the line in his behavior with a girl. I'll never have to worry that he is failing a class, not applying himself, or going to get suspended.

It's all a matter of perspective. There is always a flip side.

Two people can look at the same one thing and see two entirely different things. You can look at something and see it two ways as well. You have a choice in how you look at things. Choose well. Choose joy.

I still struggle occasionally not to go to the Dark Side at times. One of the harder aspects of our life is that we just can't simply get away for respite or a vacation like typical families. Often, you feel like there is no end to constant toil and turmoil. It's so easy to get jealous of others who can just take off at a moment's notice for rest and relaxation.

Earlier this year on our son's spring break, we decided that for the first time in five years, we would attempt a family getaway. Now, let me explain the "special needs baggage equivalency ratio." Simply put, it means that you require three bags for every day of the trip for your child with special needs. We were going to the mountains for four days, so that meant twelve bags for us!

Our trip ended up lasting less than forty-three hours.

I sat on the edge of the bed after the first day with this thought: *I think I will move to Australia.*

The young boy Alexander in Judith Vorst's award-winning children's book, *Alexander and the Terrible, Horrible, No Good, Very Bad Day*, utters those words. That was one of my personal favorite books as a child. Now here I was, sitting on the edge of the bed at 2:16 AM tempted to check the flight schedules to Sydney myself.

Five years had passed since the last time we had attempted to take a family trip together. That one had ended with me in a coma. Those were the good old days compared to this family vacation.

With Jon Alex's profound special needs, coupled with his autistic demand for routine and structure, we knew it would be a challenge to slip off for a few days together. However, the cabin was free, the drive less than three hours, and the timing seemed right, so we went for it.

Out of concern for overflowing bathtubs onto the hardwood floors, the cabin owners had made sure there was absolutely no way to stop up the tub for a bath. Baths just happen to be our son's favorite activity and part of his nightly routine. So baths were out for the duration of the trip.

There was no chair safe enough to leave him unattended, so he was forced to stay in his wheelchair for a great portion of the time in the cabin. The television set was mounted up high, which, when coupled with his vision issues, prevented him from watching his favorite videos. So quite simply, there was nothing for him to do, and his routine was getting out of sorts by the minute.

During the cold war, the United States used a scale called DEFCON to determine our state of alertness. DEFCON 5 meant we were at peace, while DEFCON 1 meant nuclear war was imminent.

At 4:00 PM that first day, I took our family's status to DEFCON 3.

Jon Alex's mobility issues put a severe limit on what he could physically do outside of the cabin environment. So going into town to find things to entertain him with was not really a viable option either.

Meanwhile, tensions were escalating rapidly inside the cabin. Our conversations were getting terse, our words sharp, and our tempers brief. Bedtime came and brought a new round of problems. The cabin only had one bedroom on the main level. With Jon Alex's cerebral palsy and my handicapped feet, we would have to find a way for all of us to sleep on the main level.

We decided to blow up a double high air mattress to put on the floor for Jon Alex to prevent him from rolling off a regular bed in the night. Despite being nonverbal, Jon Alex expressed his delight with the arrangements by turning the air mattress into his own personal trampoline. He sat cross-legged and bounced and bounced—and he bounced.

Did I mention he bounced? Not for a minute, not for a moment, not for an hour—but for the whole night! He would not go to sleep. The air mattress would lose air from all the bouncing, and he would sink towards the floor. We would have to lift him up and reinflate the mattress over and over.

Here we were now at 2:16 AM, everyone wide-awake, yet utterly exhausted.

As Alexander had said in the book, "It had been a terrible, horrible, no good, very bad day." I took our family's status to DEFCON 2, and downloaded a Visit Australia app for my smartphone.

The sun came up on day two of our unfortunate incarceration. The second day was a repeat of the first day in many ways. Tensions escalated at an alarming rate. We were beyond tired. We were bored and the thought of staying there the rest of the week was unbearable. Becky and I began throwing out trial balloons to each other about ending the vacation earlier than we had planned and just returning home. I was secretly looking at the Qantas Airlines flight schedule.

Once again, we put the air mattress down after once again forgoing the nightly bath. And once again, Jon Alex was thrilled to have his indoor trampoline back. No sleep for anyone the entire night, yet again.

I channeled Barry Corbin as General Beringer in the movie *War Games* as he said, "Flush the bombers, get the subs in launch mode, and take us to DEFCON 1."

At 10:00 PM, we decided to leave the following afternoon and return home.

At midnight, we decided to move up our departure time to noon.

At 2:00 AM, we decided to leave after breakfast.

At 4:00 AM under the cover of darkness, and pouring rain, we loaded up and made our move. Who needs breakfast anyway?

At 7:45 AM, we pulled into the driveway of home sweet home. Jon Alex soaked in the bathtub with a huge grin on his face, and I crawled under a blanket in my favorite recliner. I clicked my heels as I slipped my shoes off and said, "There's no place like home."

Once again, I had to make a choice. I could be miserable and lament the fact that we couldn't even get away for just a few days. Or, as hard as seemed at the time, I had to choose to find the humor and the lesson in the experience. I had to choose the flip side.

As long as I rely on the things of this life to sustain my joy, all things will ultimately fail me. I can have periods of happiness, but my joy can only be found in my walk with God. I will ultimately never be satisfied trying to find it in things of this world.

This week as I write this, the group Autism Speaks released the new numbers on autism as reported by the Centers for Disease Control. They report autism now affects 1 in 68 children and 1 in 42 boys.

But there is one statistic that has the most profound significance and meaning to me, and that is 1 in 1.

I have one child, and he has autism.

He also has brown hair, blue eyes, and an infectious smile. Autism no more defines him than those other characteristics define him. My son has never developed language, so we live with a completely nonverbal sixteen-year-old boy. He watches the same exact video every day at 5:00 PM (has for eleven years) and acts like he is viewing it for the first time.

He has to follow his routine, structure, and schedule relentlessly. And when his sensory environment gets overloaded, he shuts down.

Every single aspect of our lives has been affected and altered by his autism. Our dreams, our plans, our schedule, our finances, our faith, our everyday way of life all have been affected. *Autism is emotional strip mining of the soul. Nothing is left unscathed or unscarred.*

Dealing with our son's special needs has been the most challenging and demanding thing we could ever imagine. It has also been so rewarding and the biggest blessing we can imagine.

We have learned the true essence of unconditional love. We have learned what true, utter dependence on God really means. We have learned about sacrificial love, finding joy in the simple things, living life one day at a time, and treasuring every moment and every accomplishment.

We have learned so much about the nature and character of God, and we have learned so much about our relationship with each other, with God, and to the world around us.

People often ask, "Don't you wish your life was normal?" My answer is that "This is my normal." This is all I know, so this must be my normal.

Normal is what you say it is.

Our life is not dictated by our circumstances or situation. Our lives are dictated by how we choose to respond to them. Autism has robbed our family of so much in this life. And yes, it has scarred us.

But the way we have responded to it and used the experience to enrich us, teach us, and bless us has allowed God to redeem, reclaim, and restore what was stolen from us and threatened to harm us.

My son is still autistic.

He is also wonderfully made, created for a plan and a purpose, and destined to glorify God.

Have you ever been watching a movie that you have seen before, and a certain scene comes on that you really hated or was painful? Do you find yourself turning your eyes away or momentarily changing channels because you simply don't want to watch that particular scene?

I felt that way about my life towards the end of last week. We had a lot of challenges we were dealing with as a family.

Jon Alex's cerebral palsy was presenting some new medical issues, extended family members were dealing with some serious issues, and, honestly, some things occuring at work were discouraging me.

I was coming home at night feeling like everywhere I turned there was a wall of discouragement, problems, and situations that seemed to never end. We were at an event and our photographer complained that she couldn't get any good pictures of me because, in every one of them, I had a scowl on my face.

Pictures show us what is happening at a specific time, in a specific place, at a specific moment in our lives. But they don't tell our story. Sometimes I forget that.

The reason I didn't like the scenes in my life last week is because I did not understand how it would fit into the final story of my life. In the moment that you live the scenes of your life, it is impossible to see what God is going to do with the final epic manuscript of his story. The parts of my life that I find the most challenging, the most grueling, and the most despairing may just be the moments that are setting up the most incredible parts to come in the story.

What if my biggest failure became the soundstage for God to do something epic? What if my biggest weakness or limitation allowed him his biggest opportunity to use my life for his purposes? What if my biggest struggles were the biggest moments for his glory?

What if I surrendered my story to him and asked him to use my story in the telling of his greater story? We will never understand our lives by just glancing at snapshots. Only when the entire story is told will it make sense and all the scenes will come together.

Before the age of digital camera and smartphones, everyone took snapshots. You would take them to a local drugstore or store to be developed and have to pick them days later. Unless you had a state-of-the-art Polaroid instant camera!

Over time, every family accumulated box after box of old snapshots that were kept in a closet, attic, or basement.

Every once in a while, usually at some form of family get-together, the snapshots would be dragged out for a walk down memory lane. The challenge was that over time, unless you marked it on the back of the picture or saved it in an album, it became so easy to forget where and when each picture was taken.

Just looking at random snapshots doesn't reveal or explain the story of your life. God is shooting a motion picture using the universe as a screen to tell his story. So trying to understand your life by just looking at where you are now, a snapshot of a moment in time, is senseless.

You cannot dream or imagine what God is doing with your life story because you only get glimpses at snapshots. And if God let you see in advance what the story of your life was going to look like, you would probably freak out.

We never dreamed we would be changing pull-ups on our sixteen-year-old son. We never dreamed we would have to feed our child, bite by bite, for his whole life. We never dreamed we would be up several times every night, attending to him.

We never dreamed our child would need us to bathe him, dress him, change him, and care for him around the clock for the rest of our lives. We never dreamed we would never hear him talk or say one word to us.

We never dreamed he would be unable to look us in the eye for more than just a brief few seconds. We never dreamed that every aspect of our lives would be turned upside down and changed forever. We never dreamed our child would never leave home, never marry, and never give us grandkids. We never dreamed this would be our way of life.

We never dreamed we would pretty much sacrifice our hopes and dreams, and have to lay down our lives for our child.

I believe that being the parent of a child with special needs is one of the most thankless, sacrificial, emotionally draining, endlessly tiring, physically demanding, least understood roles anyone could have in life. But I also believe it can be one of the most rewarding, noble, honorable, and blessed roles anyone could have in life.

Sometimes I have to remind myself of that when my son gets up so early in the morning.

My son woke us all up with a start at 3:22 AM one morning.

It's not his fault. His autism can really mess up his sleep cycle. Not to mention he can't tell time, so when he wakes up, he assumes it is time to get up. There is no rolling back over and going back to sleep.

Sleeping in for him means making it past 5:45 on a good morning. Right now, we are in a season where his vocal stemming is out of control. So when he wakes up, the party begins! I don't mind getting up early in the morning at all. However, I would like for it to at least be "in the morning."

We are having one of those seasons those of you with children with special needs know full well. We are dealing with getting fitted for new braces on his legs and feet, trying to get a referral appointment to a GI doctor, and his sleep issues. We also both work outside the home. This week as I write this, it just seems like challenges are cropping up and piling on every day.

You may relate. This journey takes its toll emotionally, physically, financially, and relationally. You can get brittle and fragile very easily.

So you crawl into bed exhausted, too tired to think, unable to decompress at all, and wondering what on earth is going to happen next. The reality of raising a child with profound special needs is that oftentimes, you just don't get any respite, relief, or downtime. There are seasons where you feel weary to your very core. The exhaustion leaves you numb as you struggle to just go through the motions.

People will try to comfort you and say things like, "God won't give you any more than you can handle." There's a lot of comfort in that statement, but there is one thing wrong with that statement.

It's not true. It's not even in the Bible.

Oh, how we want that statement to be true! The truth is, however, that in life, you will constantly face one situation after another that you are not equipped to handle on your own.

If you could handle it all on your own, you wouldn't need God, would you? You cannot survive and make it through without relying totally and completely on him. In fact, scripture says that God says, *"My grace is sufficient for you, for my power is made perfect in weakness."* (2 Corinthians 12:9, ESV)

God is saying that in the middle of your life's greatest challenges, when you are the most vulnerable and weakest, his power becomes greatest in your life. That is the moment you have to rely on his never-ending grace. His grace says no matter how bad your past, no matter how deep the pit you are in now, and no matter how overwhelming the future seems, God still loves you deeply. That's the moment you have to realize, as Paul expressed, that his grace is sufficient for you.

Living out of grace means you shift your focus. It's no longer about eliminating the troubles in your life or taking away the challenges. Now it is about discovering and relying on the presence of God through your circumstances and trials.

Jesus says it this way, *"Come to me, all of you who are weary and carry heavy burdens, and I will give you rest. Take my yoke upon you. Let me teach you, because I am humble and gentle at heart, and you will find rest for your souls. For my yoke is easy to bear, and the burden I give you is light."* (Matthew 11:28-30)

One time, we were trying some new medicines with Jon Alex. As a result, something freaky happened with his sleep pattern. For an entire month, he would only sleep every other night. On the alternative nights, he would sit up, squeal his autistic sounds, and bounce in his bed all night long. He never would lie down and he never closed his eyes. We would try over and over at night to roll him over and get him to go to sleep, but it was to no avail.

This went on for an entire month. I was weary to my bones. I would go to work and be in a daze all day. How do you survive? How do you hold on in times or situations like that?

For me, there are a couple of things I do. I have to condition myself to take it one day at a time. It's really that simple. Live life one day at a time, or else it will get overwhelming. Jesus himself even said not to worry about tomorrow, for tomorrow will have its own troubles!

We have to learn to literally just take it one day at a time. Adopt the motto, "Improvise, adapt, and overcome." Tomorrow will have its own set of problems to face. Nothing good will come by prematurely dreading the next day.

Just laugh. Even when you don't feel like laughing, laugh anyway. If you don't learn to laugh about life, you will stay miserable. Laughter lightens the load, breaks the tension, and soothes the hurting.

Remember it's not about you. God is telling his story through your life. The story of your life isn't even about you. He chose you and has called you. He has equipped you and given your life a plan and a purpose.

Your struggles, your pain, and your challenges may be setting a huge stage for God to show his glory in triumph. The parts of your life that bring you the most pain may just be the parts he intends to use the most.

Remember that he is the God who fights for you.

"Don't be shocked or afraid of them! The Lord your God is going ahead of you. He will fight for you." (Deuteronomy 1:29-30)

Or, as God tells Joshua, *"Have I not commanded you? Be strong and courageous. Do not be frightened, and do not be dismayed, for the Lord your God is with you wherever you go."* (Joshua 1:9)

So stop right now and ask God to fight for you in your specific need at this moment. What do you do when the waves are crashing, the winds are howling, and the rain is threatening to capsize you? What do you do when God puts you in a boat you didn't choose and sets you off on a journey you don't want to take to a destination you didn't get to pick?

Stay in the boat, my friends.

The toils of raising a child with special needs can occasionally make us feel all alone. We want to go away to an isolated cave, curl up in a fetal position, close our eyes, and turn off our senses. We can find ourselves sitting in the darkness of an emotional cave, wondering how we got there and how do we get out.

I have been to that cave before and I recognize the cave. Many nights I have slept on its cold hard floors staring into the darkness.

I have rubbed my hands on its clammy walls not sure what I was feeling. I have tripped and fallen so many times while stumbling around in this cave. I have curled up like a ball in the corner looking for any source of light.

It's the autism cave. The autism cave looks just like the cerebral palsy cave. And I am familiar with both of them. They are stifling, dark, lonely caves where you feel like you can't breathe or find your way out. You sense the walls closing in on you.

I know the terrain. I know where the stalagmites are. I come here a lot. You may, too, from time to time.

And so you curl up, you sit, and you cry to yourself. You peer out sometimes looking for hope, looking for light, looking for reason. You wallow in its deepest pit and you let its grime cover your emotions.

You feel all alone. Abandoned. Tired. Distraught. Lonely.

Another year has ended, and another year has begun. But nothing else changed.

This year, still more parents will find the cave. They will learn of a diagnosis, a rare disease, a special need. They will utter those words we all remember, "What does that mean?"

Search engines will fire up. New terms and diagnoses will be researched. Thousands of parents will make an appointment with "Dr. Google."

Tears will be shed. Dreams will die. Lives will be altered forever. Then, many of them will come to the cave.

There is a beautiful story in scripture about the prophet Elijah. Elijah finds himself afraid, in despair, and feeling alone. So he runs away and hides in a cave.

The Lord comes to the edge of the cave and says to Elijah, *"What are you doing here?"*

You can almost visualize God gesturing with his hand, and then stretching out his arm to pull Elijah out of the cave.

So many new parents are going to come to the caves this year. The cluster of caves known as autism, cerebral palsy, seizures, chromosomal disorder, medically fragile, hemophilia, and Down syndrome. There are so many caves for so many special needs.

Many parents are going to want to wallow in the muck and the stench of despair. They are going to want to sit and never leave. They will feel like there is no hope. But hope must never die. Hope must never end. Sometimes hope is all you have. And when hope is all you have, hope is still enough.

As the prophet said, *"This one thing I know ... and this gives me hope. The steadfast love of God never ends."*

God comes after us when we go the cave, just like he did with Elijah. And God will stretch out his hand into the cave for you, me, and all the other special-needs parents.

And God will look into the cave and offer us his hand of hope to pull us out.

I waited patiently for the Lord
He inclined and heard my cry
He brought me up out of the pit
Out of the miry clay

I will sing, sing a new song
I will sing, sing a new song

How long to sing this song
How long to sing this song
How long ... how long ... how long...
How long ... to sing this song

He set my feet upon a rock
And made my footsteps firm
Many will see
Many will see and fear

I will sing, sing a new song
I will sing, sing a new song
I will sing, sing a new song
I will sing, sing a new song

How long to sing this song
How long to sing this song
How long ... how long ... how long...

How long ... to sing this song—

~ 40 by U2

"I will sing, sing a new song. I will sing, sing a new song."

When he was just a baby, I would hold my son Jon Alex in my arms at night and gently sing that song to him. I have no idea why that song or even how I chose that particular song. But from the moment I heard the song for the first time all those years ago, it captivated me. So it became our life song.

The lyrics that Bono wrote are based upon the 40th Psalm, which reads, *"I waited patiently for the Lord to help me, and he turned to me and heard my cry. He lifted me out of the pit of despair, out of the mud and the mire. He set my feet on solid ground and steadied me as I walked along. He has given me a new song to sing, a hymn of praise to our God. Many will see what he has done and be amazed. They will put their trust in the Lord."* (Psalm 40:1-3)

When Jon Alex began to miss milestones early in his development, I would sing over him, *"How long ... to sing this song."*

When he refused to make eye contact with anyone in his early years and acted as if we weren't even there, I would cry, *"How long ... to sing this song. How long ... how long...."*

When he couldn't talk, when he couldn't walk, when he wouldn't play with toys, when he wouldn't even acknowledge us, I would sing every night, *"How long... to sing this song."*

168

Every time we saw the pediatrician and he muttered "developmental delay," I would hear those haunting lyrics in my head.

As my vocabulary grew and I learned new words like autism, cerebral palsy, sensory processing disorder, even then, I would hold him at night and softly sing *"How long, to sing this song. How long ... how long. ... "*

Those words became my constant lament; my own personal Book of Lamentations written from my own pit where my soul lay crumbled and crushed.

I think most people have something in their lives that makes them whisper and wonder, "How long to sing this song?"

For me, it's questions such as these: Who is going to take care of my son when we are gone? Will he ever make any progress in his quality of life? Is this all there will ever be? How can we ever afford the bills? What will he do when he is out of school? Will he ever talk or even walk on his own? How is this going to affect our dreams, our goals, our lives? How will we take care of him when we are older, even elderly?

O Lord, "How long to sing this song, how long, how long?"

And so we are here tonight are in his room. His room. My sanctuary.

I call it that because I'm convinced the Spirit of God hangs out at J.A.'s place.

He is sitting cross-legged in his platform swing hanging from the ceiling. I am seated beside the swing, pushing it back and forth while singing our silly little songs that we ritualistically do in the same order every night.

The moment comes, as it does every night, when I lean over and say, "Jon Alex, you are the top dog, the big cheese, the number one son, my right hand man, crown prince, heir to the throne, the big dog, the big wave, the big kahuna, my man, my wingman, Superman."

Sounds downright goofy as I write out the words. But it's our thing. (I don't care what you think! I don't sing it to you!)

And at that very moment as I spoke, he reached his feeble arms out and wrapped them around my neck. He pulled himself to a standing position in front of me using his arms. I encircled his waist with my arms to prevent him from falling.

For six seconds that lasted six years to me, he locked in on my eyes with blazing intensity from inches away, and his gap-toothed grin split his face in two. And then he leaned in and kissed the top of my head, arms around my neck.

Flash bombs of light exploded in my heart at that very moment. How could I possibly love anyone more than this beautiful gift I had been given? What had I done that made God deem me worthy of choosing me to be this young man's father? Why did he lavish his great love on me by giving me Jon Alex to be my son?

Gratefulness, thankfulness, unspeakable love, grace, mercy, joy, peace, contentment, satisfaction, God's presence, God's provision,

God's purpose—like waves of Roman candles on the Fourth of July, they came shooting out of the bottom of the pit.

The cold floor of the pit suddenly grew warm. I could no longer feel the miry clay, for my feet had been set upon a rock. The Rock. God had heard my cry. He lifted me up out of the pit, out of the miry clay. And I began to sing the rest of the song.

"I will sing, sing a new song. I will sing, sing a new song."

Pulling into the driveway one day before last Christmas, I saw Becky emerging through the opening garage door. In an instant, I knew she had finally received the phone call we were both looking forward to and yet dreading at the same time.

"Vanderbilt Children's just called. The test shows he is having seizures," she said softly. I could tell she had been crying.

For the past sixteen years, we have wrestled with Jon Alex's special needs—autism, cerebral palsy, mental and cognitive impairment, and lack of mobility. We have grieved over and over. We have wrestled with God for answers. And yet somehow through all the storms, we have stayed the course.

But recently, Jon Alex had been exhibiting some new behaviors that concerned us. The neurologists had suggested some tests. We learned from the tests that Jon Alex now has epileptic seizures, in addition to his other special needs.

Getting a new diagnosis stirs up all those old emotions. The grief cycle begins again, and what was the new normal gives way to the even newer normal. The Dark Side beckoned again.

I wanted to shout out, "Why God? Why now?" I wanted to scream and kick and complain. But then I reminded myself what I espouse so often to others to whom I minister.

God is telling his story through my son's life. None of this is about me, or us, or my son. This is the part we have been given in his story. When I cry out "It's not fair," I remind myself that grace isn't fair either, though. I don't deserve grace, but he gives it to me anyway.

God's will and plan is that everything he does brings more people into his kingdom. His word promises to take care of the faithful believer in the end. And we can stand on the assurance that in all things, he will be glorified and worthy of honor.

So when I accept my role in his story and I realize it's his story we are writing in the first place, I see things differently. I have hope. Hope that anchors my soul. Hope that God will use this journey we are on to accomplish those three things.

The day will come when there will be no more crying and no more tears. There will be no more pain and no more sorrow. God says he himself will wipe them away and he will make all things new.

Autism will be defeated.
Cerebral palsy will no longer exist.
Seizures will cease.

Death will be no more.
Sorrow will turn into joy and mourning into dancing.
The last chapter of the story will be revealed.

When hope is all you have, hope will be enough. Because when hope is all you've got, you've got all you need.

There is a moving account in scripture where the prophet Jeremiah approaches God. He begins to list a long litany of complaints against God. He basically says, if I can paraphrase, *"I didn't choose this path for my life, you did, God. And all I've seen since then is suffering. I've had one trial after another trial. Now my life is full of despair. I can't go on like this any longer. I have lost my hope. I have lost my will to live. You did this to me and now I am tired, hurting, and discouraged."*

Many nights in the early days of our journey with Jon Alex, I thought or did the same thing.

But an interesting thing happens to Jeremiah as he stands in the presence of God. He lists his complaints, and then slowly as he basks in God's presence, his attitude begins to shift. He concludes by saying that he still calls the Lord to mind, and for this reason he has hope.

"The faithful love of the Lord never ends! His mercies never cease. Great is his faithfulness; his mercies begin afresh each morning. I say to myself, "The Lord is my inheritance; therefore, I will hope in him!" (Lamentations 3:22-24, ESV)

My own hope is built on nothing less as well.

The Dark Side is just a place you will encounter throughout your journey. But it is just a pit stop, not a final destination. The Dark Side doesn't require a passport to visit, as long as you don't take up residence.

Chapter 11
THRIVING, NOT JUST SURVIVING

When our son was an infant, too young for an autism diagnosis, we were already noticing the developmental delays. There was a season where doctors were sure something was different, but not yet ready to give it a label because of his age.

I remember stealing a glance at his medical chart on one such visit and I noted the diagnosis code written on the charts. I called my sister who is a nurse practitioner and asked her to look the code up for me.

I can still hear the words as she said, *"Failure to thrive."* Even now as I type the words out, they still seem to echo in my head.

The phrase "failure to thrive" conjures up so many destructive emotions. At the time, I was absolutely crushed.

When I look around our special-needs community today, I see so many families like ours that I would diagnose as "failure to thrive." They are desperately trying to hold on, clinging to their emotional, spiritual, mental, and even physical well-being.

The stresses of raising a child with special needs, combined with the routine stresses of this world, are so amplified in their lives that they are barely surviving.

They struggle to make it from day-to-day, riding a roller coaster of emotions. They often accept their lives on face value as being as good as it gets. With marriages on edge, struggling financially, and emotionally spent, they survive one day at a time.

I realized that if my family was going to not just survive but also actually thrive, I was going to have to be willing to quit trying to control everything and become utterly dependent on God. That meant ridding myself of pride and arrogance and surrendering to God completely. Not surrendering and still doubting God are just signs of personal arrogance.

I am a self-admitted control freak. For most of my married life, I have always insisted on driving us. Anytime we were going somewhere together, I always drove. Even if I were going somewhere with friends or coworkers, I insisted on driving.

I liked being in control. I liked determining the route and controlling the situation, speed, and path to our destination.

Thanks to my broken right foot and resulting damage a couple of years ago, I had to begin letting Becky drive whenever we went anywhere. For several months while in a cast, she had to chauffeur me around everywhere I went.

I hated it at first.

She drives differently from me. She takes different routes from what I would choose. I'm not in control anymore. She dictates the speed, the path, the timing, and the route. At first, I would pout and say things like, "Why are you going this way?" Or I would say, "Slow down," or "I don't like going this way, let's go the route I always go."

I just couldn't handle not being in control anymore. I want to adjust the mirrors, arrange the seats, pick the radio station, determine the routes, decide how fast we go and when we stop. I want to monitor the gas, pick my speed, steer the wheel, and guide the car.

I really need to learn from my son Jon Alex.

When Jon Alex was young, we would put him in the car, and he would just settle back to enjoy the ride. He never questioned the destination. He never questioned the route. He didn't even ask where we were going or care how we got there. He just sat back and enjoyed the ride. Whether it was sunny or stormy, it didn't matter with him.

He's content to go to whatever destination we go and pays no matter to how we get there. He just trusts me. Detours don't faze him. He has no interest in being in control or even knowing what's going on or where we're headed. He just sits in the backseat and lets dad handle the rest. By doing so, he rides along in complete peace.

I tend to live my life like I drive. I want to steer the wheel. I want to decide where I'm going in life and how I'm going to get there. I want to determine the pace of my life and be in control.

I want to plan my own life and control every aspect of it.

The reality is that God wants me to be like Jon Alex. God wants me to slip into the backseat and enjoy the ride while letting him take care of the rest. God wants me to trust him completely and surrender control.

"*Let me drive,*" he whispers.

Jon Alex has it figured out. I could learn a lot from him.

Now that Jon Alex is older, we have to make a decision every morning. Front seat or back seat?

His mom drives him across the town to our local high school and drops him off for school. Then, in the afternoon, she chauffers him back home from school.

Jon Alex loves riding in the car. Unfortunately, his motives for wanting to ride are sometimes not the best.

With his combination of autism and cerebral palsy, being strapped in the seat gives him his own playground for movement. He leans up as far as the safety belt allows, and then deliberately hurls himself back into the seat. Over and over and over he does this, and he does it repetitively as fast as he can.

Somehow his movement-starved body has turned our car into his own personal amusement park. The stares we receive at traffic lights are priceless. Strangers peer into the car with their jaws open. Sometimes other kids point. When we are parked and he starts rocking, the entire vehicle just shakes. People pass by and I slump over in the seat hiding behind my sunglasses.

He cannot help the behavior. It's just a part of his autism. Because he is so mobility impaired, I understand his craving and I take delight that he can rock like that in the car. It satisfies that craving to be able to control his own movement, and he has figured out it is safe as long as he is buckled in the seat. He rocks so much he actually broke the seat in our minivan last year.

Ask any parent of a child with autism; we can usually tell by the morning routines what the day may hold based upon the events that morning. In our house, we call it having a special-needs moment.

As a result, some mornings Jon Alex is far more hyper and wound up than others. He is vocally and physically stimming away constantly. We stand him up and he begins stomping his feet, making it terribly difficult to walk him to the car.

That's when we have to make the decision. Front seat or back seat?

He is sixteen and loves riding in the front seat with Mom. But in the front seat, there's a greater chance of him hitting his head on the dashboard or window and even flailing so wildly it distracts my wife who is driving. He might even reach over towards the controls. The backseat doesn't have those issues and gives him more freedom of movement. So we have to choose each day where he rides.

Every morning, you and I have to make a similar decision as it relates to God.

Will we be content to let God drive us where we are going that day and ride along quietly in the backseat? Will we let him choose the course and direction while allowing him to steer without our attempting to take the wheel? Will we trust that he knows how to drive the car without our help, and allow ourselves to sit back and enjoy the trip?

Or will we try to get God to let us sit in the front seat where we are tempted to try to take over the controls, determine the course, or suggest what path we would like him to take?

What kind of passenger will you be today?

If I'm going to survive this journey, then I have to let go of my desire to try to control every situation and manage it myself. If I truly want to thrive, I have to surrender that control to God and let him drive my life, trusting him at the controls. By my own power I may survive, but Jesus said he came not just to give us life, but abundant life. In other words, not just so we can survive, but so we can thrive in any situation.

Several years ago, I started having some trouble with my eyes due to lack of oxygen getting where it needed to go. The condition led to bleeding in my eyes that became quite severe.

Right before Christmas that year, I had to undergo eye surgery. The postoperative recovery plan called for me to keep my head in a certain position for a few days while my eye healed. I felt like a bat hanging from the ceiling for several days as I recovered. I thought I would go crazy. The days seemed to last forever. I was miserably uncomfortable all the time.

Finally one night when it just seemed like sleep would be impossible, I crawled out of bed and sat in a chair in the corner of our bedroom with my head bowed towards the ground as instructed, waiting for morning to come. I found myself praying under my breath for relief. I moaned and expressed my frustration and weariness. And in the quiet that is the middle of the night, I felt alone.

Too tired to think, too uncomfortable to sleep, and too afraid to make any noise, I just sat in the dark.

That's when it happened. An overwhelming peace just enveloped me as I sensed God whispering, *"I'm here."* No promise of relief, no assurances of change, and no healing from my circumstances. Just a gentle reminder of his presence. Just a simple declaration from the voice that spoke the stars into existence.

"I'm here."

That was enough. Just to know I wasn't alone. Just to know he was walking through it with me. That was all I needed to know in order to find peace.

It reminded me so much of my interaction with Jon Alex.

Because he is nonverbal, he can't tell us when something is wrong. So if he gets upset at night, all he can do is cry for us to hear him. Because he's my son, I race to his side and as soon as I'm there, I declare, "Dad's here, I'm here, Jon Alex."

And even though he only hears "I'm here," what he really hears is, "Dad's here now, I will protect you, comfort you, guard you, watch over you, and love you. You don't have to be afraid."

That's what those simple words really imply and mean. So go ahead.

Whatever is robbing your peace, whatever is stealing your joy, whatever is threatening to overwhelm you, close your eyes and listen for the voice of God to simply declare, "I'm here."

I had an operation in both eyes to help repair the damage and prevent the issue from happening again. Unfortunately, one of the side effects of the procedure I had done is that it caused the rapid development of cataracts. A cataract is a milky, cloudy effect that makes vision difficult because it's like looking through a fog or cloud to see. I kept trying to clean my glasses, only to realize there was nothing on my glasses.

The problem was in my eye.

I had surgery to remove the cataract. The surgeon drained the problem in the eye and implanted a new lens in my eye. Now when I look at something, I'm looking through a new clear lens. The surgery itself took less than ten minutes.

Don't you wish you could clear up the cloudy, dirty lens we view the world through and exchange it for a new lens in the same little amount of time?

See, I'm guilty of trying to view people—their intentions and motives, their manners and personalities, their position and value—through my jaded, cynical, tired, old lens. I've let scar tissue build up from old wounds, old battles, old hurts, and old trials and circumstances. So my view is always cloudy, always skeptical, always impaired so to speak.

I've developed spiritual cataracts.

I think we let our unresolved emotions, hurts and pain, and life experiences build up in our eyes like cataracts, and we need God to give us a new lens, a new perspective to view the world. That's been one of my prayers for this year. God let me see people as you see them. Help me value every single person and life like you do. God, let me look through your lens at everyone.

Exchanging judgment for grace, dropping conditional love and acceptance for unconditional love and wholeheartedness. Helping me celebrate the goodness and individuality in people, and making me blind to what divides and separates.

Give me a new lens to look through.

I think that's something we all could use. I wish I could have always been like that, even when I was a child still in school. I wish I had better spiritual lenses back then as well. I will never forget the next story.

He would stand off in the corner of the room, two fingers shoved in his mouth, while he played with glue. The class bully would go over and dare him to eat the glue. Eyes wide and shaking his head, nevertheless, he would eventually comply and stick a huge amount of the glue into his mouth.

I can still remember the class bully laughing, pointing, and taunting while the rest of the class looked on in disgust.

He was desperate for friendship, desperate to feel like he belonged, and desperate to just be one of the gang. So he would tag along, always lingering a couple of steps behind everyone else. He always seemed to be the butt of everyone else's jokes.

He obviously had special needs. It was obvious he was both physically and intellectually challenged. And for a private school made up of mostly educators' children from a nearby university, it was obvious he wasn't like the other kids.

The class bully would pretend to buddy up to him, but too often his intent was to make this boy with special needs the victim of a cold or cruel joke. Oh, the humiliation he underwent every day.

A couple of years later, a similar situation developed with another boy. Everyone could see what was going to happen next. That same bully, one of the most popular boys in the school, at this point began to pick on this boy with special needs as well. And because of the bully's popularity, the rest of the class took their cue from him and began to behave the same way.

That poor boy with special needs just wanted to be like everyone else. But everyone else didn't leave school crying bitterly every day like he did.

Even though those memories are now thirty-eight years old, I can still remember them so vividly today.

Part of why those memories affect me so much is because I'm now the father of a boy with special needs myself. I can't imagine what I would feel and how I would react if that happened to my son with special needs.

Part of why those memories affect me so much is because I'm a missionary to the special needs community, and I see the effects of bullying every day though our ministry.

But mostly, those memories affect me so much and seem so vivid because I was the bully.

I have always believed as God says in Psalm 139 that God wrote all of the days of my life in his book before one of them came to pass. That means that in the mid-1970s when I was a bully to those with special needs, God had already chosen me to be his ambassador or missionary to the special-needs community.

And even though God had ordained it before I was ever born, it still seems inconceivable that the bully would grow up and feel like God was calling him to give his life to serve those with special needs.

But then I think about the apostle Paul, who God had already chosen to be his apostle, even while Paul (still known as Saul) was murdering those who followed Christ.

Two years ago, I decided to track down the first boy in this story. I couldn't remember the other kid's name, but I remembered the first boy and I wanted to see him face-to-face. I wanted to apologize to him these thirty-eight years later. I wanted his forgiveness. I needed him to know what I had done with my life and that I was atoning for those childhood years. I needed him to know that who I was in grade school was not who I was anymore.

Through Internet searches and sources I found him, still here in my hometown where we went to school together.

I found him buried in a local cemetery, having died in 1995 when he was twenty-eight years old.

I stood at his grave and I sobbed. I cried for who I had been and what I had done all those years ago. I had come to his grave seeking healing, forgiveness, and atonement. I wanted to leave it there.

In that moment, the Spirit of God whisked me away in my thoughts and mind to another grave. All of a sudden, in my mind I was in front of a cave outside Jerusalem, near a skull-shaped hill called Golgotha.

In that instant, God spoke to me and reminded me that this was the real grave where my forgiveness, atonement, and healing were to be found. And, as a result, I am not who I used to be. That's not who I am now.

"Just leave it here," he whispered.

Though my past indiscretions were close to forty years old, my forgiveness and deliverance from them was actually purchased for me in advance over 2,000 years ago.

I know so many people struggling today to let go of past struggles, despair, disappointment, guilt, bitterness, and anger. I see so many people haunted by who they used to be. I see people who can't move forward because they are still struggling carrying around baggage from their past.

It's time to go to the gravesite. It's time to gaze upon the empty tomb and guzzle from the cup of grace until it runs down your chin.

And it's time to listen to him whisper, "That's not who you are anymore."

It's time to leave it at the empty grave. Just leave it there.

Grace is how God makes the unforgivable forgivable.

Every parent of a school-age child with special needs is intimately familiar with the IEP. I will never forget our first IEP meeting. I had no idea what to expect and certainly no idea of what was about to happen.

The room was full of early intervention therapists, school therapists, service providers, teachers, and administrators. I'm pretty sure I even met the governor and the secretaries of Transportation and

Veteran's Affairs! I looked around the room and felt like I was testifying before Congress.

This year, we met for our son's thirteenth IEP. That thought made me think. *What if God did an IEP on each one of us every year?*

What if you got summoned to the throne room of heaven once a year for God to complete an IEP on you?

"Thanks for coming in today, Mr. Davidson. My name is Michael. Let me introduce you to the others here today. This is the LORD GOD, and to his right is Jesus Christ. I believe you two met when you were eleven years old, Jeff."

I notice that in front of God is a huge file folder with my name written across it in a beautiful calligraphy. God opens the file and began to speak.

"I'd like to start by discussing Jeff's strengths and positive characteristics we've observed. He has a wonderful sense of humor and works well with others. He stays motivated and has a vivid sense of imagination.

"Our evaluations show he tests well in transparency, and he shows real improvement in valuing those like him as well as those not like him. We have moved his mercy ranking from a 3 to a 4 based upon his performance this year. He demonstrated practically no mercy at all several years ago, so the direct services have helped him make great strides in that area.

"Our testing reveals a real aptitude for leadership, administration, and teaching, putting him in the upper quadrant.

"However, our real life observations in the field also show some serious deficiencies and areas he continues to lag far behind that we need to address.

"Jeff continues to place a much higher value on receiving grace than he does on giving grace to others. He also continues to struggle with pride, envy, and jealousy.

"His latest evaluations show he can be judgmental and quick-tempered. Right now, we are just looking at this on a consultative basis, but if it doesn't improve, we may have to start providing direct services once a week," God concluded.

At that moment, Jesus spoke up, *"I'm here today representing Jeff as his advocate.. Can I see the file please?"* Michael noted all this into my folder and slid it across the table to Jesus.

Jesus scribbled something on the front page, although I couldn't make it out from across the table. Then he slid the folder back to God, who opened it and glanced at the front page.

God then turned in my direction and announced that there had been a revision made to my IEP.

"A provider has stepped up and agreed to cover all your deficiencies and make up for all the areas you are lacking. Based upon his review of the file, we deem you perfect in our standing. He has

agreed to add your scores together with his own so now you have a spotless record."

Michael handed me my heavenly IEP back for my signature. As I scribbled my name, I noticed my file now only contained one page. The rest had disappeared. I snuck a glance at the page as I signed my name.

The word *"Mine"* was written boldly in blood across the page right above the scrawled signature of Jesus himself.

And then I looked at the name on the file. Jesus had marked through my name, again with his blood, and had written his own name on the front of the file where mine used to be.

Michael grinned at me as we walked out and whispered, *"No matter how often I see him do that, it never gets old!"*

"My dear children, I am writing this to you so that you will not sin. But if anyone does sin, we have an advocate who pleads our case before the Father. He is Jesus Christ, the one who is truly righteous." (1 John 2:1)

I want to remind you of some things you will need to remember to help you survive each day. There was a time when God's people were facing what they thought were insurmountable obstacles themselves. God had promised them land of their own that was "flowing with milk and honey."

So God's people sent twelve spies into the land to scout it out for them. Almost all of the spies returned trembling and afraid. *"There are giants in the land. We can't take possession of the land God promised. They are too strong for us to overcome."*

One man named Caleb then stood up in front of all the people and said that they would be able to overcome this, and they would be able to take possession of the land. He said this because he knew God would go before them and fight for them. God had promised to go with them every step of the way, and Caleb had the faith to believe in God's promises.

You are going to face giants in your land every day as a parent of a child with special needs. Every day, you are going to wonder, *How am I going to handle this today?* You will have some doubts, moments of discouragement, and fear.

The giants you face in your special-needs world are going to wake up today. Go ahead and punch them in the face and remember what God says.

God is with you on this journey. More than anything, you need to realize that you are not alone. You cannot conquer the special-needs giants in your life by your own strength and power. But with God, no giant is undefeatable. You will be more than conquerors and you will not just survive, you will actually thrive!

During some moments, you may feel all alone.

Remember, he chose you, he called you, and he equipped you. He will lead you, he will guide you, he will comfort you, and he will provide for you.

He will sustain you, he will carry you, he will redeem you, and he will restore you.
He will refresh you. He will go before you and he will go alongside you.
He will go behind you, and he will even sing over you.
But the one thing he will never do is leave you alone.

You are never alone!

The world will tell you to just give up and surrender. It will tell you that you can't do this, that you are being punished and you have no value or significance.

God's voice will tell you that he created you for a plan and a purpose, that you are wonderfully made, and that you are destined to bring him glory. You will become whatever you believe. And what you believe will be determined by whose voice you listen to.

Choose to listen to the one who made you, called you, and chose you.

Listen to God who says, *"When you pass through the waters, I will be with you; and through the rivers, they shall not overwhelm you; when you walk through fire you shall not be burned, and the flame shall not consume you."* (Isaiah 43:2, ESV)

Finally, I just want to remind you again, as I so often have stressed, that God is telling his story and has given each of you a story. But the story of your life isn't about you. God is telling his story through you. When those special needs moments come up, and they will, remember that he chose you for this part. If you allow him to control the story, you will find moments of peace, joy, and blessings along the way. But it is your choice as to what perspective to take for your journey.

Chapter 12
THE STORY ISN'T OVER

"No deposit, no return."

My father-in-law whispered those words to me as he gave me his daughter's hand at our wedding.

My wife and I have been married twenty-three years now.

I don't know if I believe in love at first sight, but I do believe in love at two weeks.

We had only been dating for two weeks and I knew Becky and I were going to get married. I tested the waters by whispering, *"I think I'm falling in love with you."*

I threw that *"I think"* in there to give myself a little wiggle room in case it didn't work out, but in my heart I knew.

We went to a fireworks show casually with some friends one night right after we met. They tell me the show was spectacular. I don't remember anything about the show. The fireworks in my head and heart drowned them out.

We got engaged in three months. I kind of failed and forgot to tell my parents I was dating anyone until we took them out for dinner. I introduced them to Becky and said we were getting married.

I probably should have thought that one through a little more. I took my future father-in-law to lunch to ask his permission to marry his daughter. He knew the reason for the lunch, but he made me sweat and mumble all through lunch just the same before smiling and welcoming me to the family.

He was marrying off his third daughter in a little over a year, so I suspect he was just getting a little revenge for the financial toil we were all taking on him.

Twenty-three years.

A lot has happened since that Saturday afternoon on May 18, 1991. When we got married, we planned on me having a successful business career and climbing the corporate ladder. Becky was going to teach school for a while. Then when the time was right, she would stay home to raise our children and we would live in a big house in the suburbs. We would lead a perfect life in a perfect world as the perfect family.

It was, in fact, a perfect plan in my eyes, because I came up with the plan. When you recite traditional wedding vows, there is always that phrase, *"for better or worse."* We took that vow as part of our wedding ceremony. Like everyone else, though, we only focused and assumed on the "better."

Have you ever noticed the "better" always gets mentioned first? The "worse" is almost thrown on like an afterthought in wedding vows.

Since that day twenty-three years ago, my plan has been totally thrown upside down.

We lost our first child to a miscarriage.

I was across the country on a business trip when it happened and was not home when my wife needed me the most.

Our second child Jon Alex has profound special needs. His cerebral palsy and autism have left him as a now sixteen-year-old boy completely nonverbal, unable to walk, and completely dependent upon us 24/7 for care.

He requires our absolute constant attention and care for everything. Over the course of his life, he has never been able to say even one word.

No one can prepare you for the grueling, exhausting, draining task of caring for a child with profound special needs. You will never attempt anything harder in your life. And it will affect everything about your life—emotionally, financially, spiritually, relationally, and mentally.

The toll it takes on your marriage is staggering.

We learned a whole new vocabulary. We learned new words like sensory processing disorder, occupational therapy, physical therapy, quadriplegia, and so forth. We learned a bunch of new acronyms as well, like IEP, AFO, EMU, and CFGF.

This was not the plan.

Nothing has gone according to my plan. But everything has gone according to God's plan.

Our twenty-three years of experiences, sixteen with our special-needs son, have been richly rewarding, richly enriching, and left us richly blessed. We are stronger, more determined, more together, and more incredibly blessed through our life than we can imagine. What should have divided us has instead united us.

What was intended to harm us has, once again by God's grace and plan, been redeemed and reclaimed for good according to his purposes.

Turns out that God's plan was the perfect one.

For all of you parents just coming to terms with a diagnosis, for all you parents just beginning this special needs journey, for all of you who right now are besieged by mixed emotions, I have one more point.

For all of you in the midst of the struggle … for all you moms and dads about to throw in the towel and quit … for all of you ready to just give up and walk away … for all of you wondering if it ever gets better … for all of you struggling to find anything good about your circumstances.

Sometimes better follows worse.

The reality is that so many of our special-needs families are failing these days. Too often, it is the dad who withdraws and ultimately leaves. But for whatever reason, the stresses are so fierce that it impacts a marriage brutally.

Communication fades, conflicts escalate, and both parties begin to feel neglected by the other. Time alone seems impossible, respite is fleeting, and you live in a world of little sleep, little rest, and little time for each other.

We have to constantly remind ourselves that we are a team. We stand back-to-back in all things. We have to choose never to become a statistic. To me it's pretty simple.

I took a vow before God. All that better or worse, sickness and in health—those weren't just words to recite. I made a covenant not just with my wife, but also with God. There were three parties in my vow.

I take my cue from the Gospel of John. No, I don't mean *that* Gospel of John. I'm talking about the one espoused by my friend John.

John and Ruth had been married for sixty-two years.

Their son and daughter-in-law had been friends of ours for many years. We knew their son, their grandchildren, and even recently their great-grandchildren.

We didn't know John and Ruth until they moved to Cookeville a few years ago and began attending our church. Ruth was in poor health so they had moved to our town to live near their son and daughter-in-law who could help care for them.

Every Sunday, John would meet her at the nursing home and drive to our church in their van. He would pull right up close to the front door. I would then watch them come in as John pushed Ruth's specially-designed hospital bed. The ushers would clear a space so they could sit in the back to be comfortable, have room, and not be a distraction.

I would watch as John doted on Ruth and attended to her every need. He would smile at her and touch her lovingly even though her health made it difficult, if not impossible, for her to respond. Occasionally he would wipe her chin or stroke her hair. I was moved by his affection and love for his wife of sixty-two years. I was captivated by the dignity and grace he displayed with her.

Clearly, he loved her with an everlasting love.

The day came when Ruth went home to see Jesus. He, too, had loved her with an everlasting love. At the funeral home, I spoke to John about how much I admired him for the way he cared so much for his wife in her latter years as I had watched the two of them.

"I took a vow," John told me. "In sickness and health I promised." What he told me next absolutely stunned me.

When John made that vow, he had no idea that for fifty of their sixty-two years together, Ruth would suffer from multiple sclerosis. For fifty years, Ruth's health would be afflicted and ravaged by MS. John walked through it side-by-side with her because, as he said, "I took a vow."

Every day I see couples on the verge of packing it in and giving up on each other. People are losing their jobs, their retirement, their homes, their faith, and their hope. Every day, we, like so many other special-needs families, struggle to cope and survive together with the unique challenges we face.

I counsel couples whose marriages are on the brink after only a few years together. I see so many couples that just can't commit to or grasp the idea of dying to themselves. And I see the stress of raising a child with special needs tear apart or threaten to destroy marriages. I see people just walking away.

Then, every once in a while, you'll meet a John and Ruth.

Sixty-two years of marriage. Fifty years of disease. Sixty-two years of love, joy, devotion, compassion and kindness—all to the very end.

Because John took a vow. And that's the gospel according to John.

Thank you, John. We needed to hear and see that.

I wish that the thirty-year-old me with the newly diagnosed son had known the now forty-seven-year-old me with a son with special needs. I wish the thirty-year-old me could have heard me say, *"This journey is going to be the hardest journey you can imagine. But it's going to be one of the most richly rewarding experiences of your life."*

I would tell him there is purpose in the pain. There will be a message in the mess, and every trial will produce a triumph. I would tell him if he surrenders his pain to God, then God will reveal himself to him in unspeakable ways.

Last year, I received a phone call from a dad who just learned of his child's special needs. We arranged to meet for a soft drink at an Arby's near his home. I soon realized I was sitting across the table from a younger version of myself in so many ways.

As I listened to him open up and share what he felt and how this news was affecting him, I couldn't help but think, *This guy is me fifteen years ago*. I could anticipate his every statement. I knew the next question he was going to ask. His every emotion, his every doubt, his every fear, his every thought—I was hearing my own story through his mouth.

He thinks this wasn't the plan. This isn't what he chose for his life or the path he would have taken. He's angry, he's bitter, he's discouraged, and he's looking for someone to blame. He is torn between blaming God and blaming himself. And he feels so alone.

He had run into a mutual acquaintance of ours who he had not seen in over twenty years. This friend had told him a little bit about me and my story. So here we were now, sitting across the table from each other in a fast-food restaurant. We talked for quite a while. I didn't try to answer any of the questions going through his mind. Not yet.

As we continue to meet and get to know each other, I'll begin to share with him a little more about how God called him to this and has chosen him. I'll teach him that his child was created for a plan and a purpose. And I'll talk about the God who is going to use his child and their story for his glory.

I will help him see his child as his greatest gift and biggest blessing. I'll help him thrive even though this new journey is going to be extremely challenging and difficult. I will show him that normal is whatever you decide normal is. I'll reveal to him that the greatest gifts are the unexpected ones. And the best plans are the ones ordained in heaven, not the ones dreamed up on earth.

I will show him that in all due time. But not right now.

Right now, he just needs to realize a couple of simple truths, and so I chose to focus on two things with him.

1) "You aren't alone. There is a whole community of us out there and we are here for one another, and for you."

2) "I'm fifteen years further down this path than you, and I'm here to tell you it's going to be OKAY. Not easy, but fulfilling in its own way. You're going to be OKAY."

In looking back at myself fifteen years ago; that's what I wish someone would have taught me. That's what I needed to hear and cling to when it happened to me.

And so that's where I started with him. And when he is ready to receive the other stuff, I'll begin by telling him of a God who loves him so much that he orchestrated a run-in with an old acquaintance of his who just so happened to know of me and gave me a call.

I will tell him of a God who purposed to put me in the chair across the table from him so that I could help him find his own purpose. A God who used my son's disability—my son's cerebral palsy and autism—and my son's life to help me discover my own purpose in life.

Because in another fifteen years, someone else is going to start down the path of raising a child with special needs. And that new dad is going to be overwhelmed and desperately needs help.

And my hope is that my new friend is going to sit across the table from him and say, "You are not alone. I'm fifteen years further down this path from you, and it's going to be OKAY. Let me tell you what an older dad once told me when I first started this journey."

In 1864, a young Catholic priest named Father Damien arrived on the coast of Hawaii as a missionary. The government of Hawaii had issued a government-sanctioned medical quarantine of leprosy patients on the Hawaiian island of Molokai.

There, in isolation, the leper patients lived, worked, and ultimately died in their own community, cut off from the rest of the population.

Father Damien moved into the leper colony and lived and worked among its people for sixteen years. He became their spiritual leader in short time. Even more so, he ministered to them spiritually, emotionally, and physically. He helped them build houses, grow food, dig graves, and assisted with basic medical needs.

He became known as the spiritual patron to the outcasts. He wrote home to his brother shortly after his arrival, saying, "I make myself a leper to gain all for Christ."

Father Damien eventually contracted the deadly disease himself, becoming a leper. One account has him shortly thereafter standing in the pulpit of the church he helped them build, and beginning his sermon by saying, "We lepers."

I always thought that one of the things that made me effective in disability ministry was that I am myself the father of a son with profound special needs. I have always felt that I was blessed with perspective to understand the feelings, needs, and mind-set of the special-needs community since our family is going through that journey ourselves.

After all, who better to minister to people with a drinking problem than a recovered alcoholic himself? Who better to minister to someone who has lost a spouse, been in an abusive relationship, or battled addiction than someone who has walked the same path? So who better to minister to the special-needs community than a dad of one himself?

But just a few years ago, I developed an issue with the bones in both of my feet. I had to have operations on both of them. The first surgery had some complications that ended up with a staph infection that put me into respiratory arrest.

I was placed on life support for several days in a medically-induced coma. A ventilator kept me alive and my wife was braced for the worst. Weeks later, I was finally released from the hospital to return home.

As I mentioned earlier in the book, I was confined to a wheelchair and limited in what I could do. I was completely dependent on others for everything in my life. Becky had to give me medicines throughout the day, prepare my meals, bathe me, dress me, and assist me with the most basic functions. I was hooked up to a machine, given IV drugs every six hours through a port on my arm, and doing daily breathing treatments to heal my lungs.

I had to learn to walk again, but this time I had to learn on feet that are now permanently deformed. I have to wear specially designed custom shoes and orthotics, and I still limp. The months in a wheelchair with no independence have gave me a whole new perspective on what it must be like to have a physical disability.

I still get frustrated, angry, and depressed sometimes with my physical limitations and the things I can no longer do. Every once in a while, I stare at my crippled feet at night and I have a little pity party. Why did this have to happen?

But, in the mornings, I watch my son gingerly walking on his own twisted feet ravaged by cerebral palsy, clinging to his mother who is holding onto him for assistance. He, too, wears braces and special shoes.

I look at his twisted, mangled feet. Then I look down on my own deformed feet. And in that moment, my mind flashes to the cross, and I'm fixated on the image of Christ's feet, with gaping bloody holes from the nails that were driven in his feet. I'm reminded that he took my beating, bore my curse, and died my death for me. All of a sudden, my disabled feet issues seems so trivial.

I watch Jon Alex every step as Becky guides him, helping him. He cannot walk unless she stands him up, holds him, and guides him. Then I look up from his twisted feet to his face and realize he is grinning ear to ear. He always seems to be grinning.

He squeals his happy sounds as she maneuvers him to his breakfast chair. And then I am humbled and I have to repent. Why can't I rise above my own disability like my son? Why is he so happy despite his condition? Once again, I am the pupil, and my son has become the teacher.

I now not only have the experience of raising an individual with special needs, but because of my own disability, I also have that perspective as well. I remind myself of the letter Father Damien wrote to his brother, and I paraphrase it in my head as it relates to me.

"I have become myself disabled to gain all for Christ."

God has broken me in more ways than I can count. And all of a sudden, my perspective is growing every day. I bear my own scars emotionally and now physically. It amplifies the meaning and significance of why Jesus had to come to earth and live with us before dying for us.

He had to live it himself. Every day. He understood everything— every emotion, every feeling, everything you and I experience. He walked it himself. He suffered pain, trials, and experiences for himself while on earth to accomplish God's purposes.

This ordeal has nothing to do with me. I was simply chosen by God as his instrument. This ordeal is about bringing more people into his kingdom. This ordeal is to advance his purposes, honor his name, and draw more people to him.

If you think about it, the point at which Jesus most glorified God was when he was hanging on the cross. As he hung there suffering, in excruciating pain, bearing the sins of the world on his back, God's glory was on full display for the entire world.

His suffering on the cross was the stage from which God's master plan for reconciling his people to him was displayed. He hung there with your pain, with your wounds, with your struggles, with your suffering, and he glorified God.

God's desire for you and me, by the way we live our lives and in everything we do, is to become Christlike. Your wounds, trials, and suffering can be your stage for God to be glorified in your life as well, as you become more Christlike. God will always meet you where your life hurts the most.

Towards the beginning of this book, I mentioned a season in our life when we had to pay someone each week to accompany us to church and attend to Jon Alex. It was the only way we could attend church together as a family. At the time, I felt so discouraged and so frustrated that we had to do that just to attend church. Now, I need to tell you the rest of the story. The rest of the story can best be summed up by two of the most powerful words ever uttered:

"But God."

Every story has a "but God." Every challenge, every struggle, every trial has an opportunity for a "but God" moment. In the story I mentioned earlier from Genesis 50, after all the hell on earth Joseph endured, after all the misery and pain, Joseph says, *"You intended to harm me, but God intended it all for good. He brought me to this position so I could save the lives of many people."* (Genesis 50:20)

There it is. *"But God."*

When the Dark Side beckons, when you feel overwhelmed, discouraged, and all alone, remember those two powerful words, "but God."

The lady we hired to be Jon Alex's buddy at church was Connie. Connie was a classroom assistant who worked with him in his classroom at school. She was his one-on-one assistant and was already so familiar with Jon Alex's ways. He was comfortable around her and they already had a bond.

Connie would meet us in the lobby every Sunday morning and take Jon Alex to class to serve as his buddy. She would often talk about how he was such a light in her life, and that just being around him brightened up her day. Connie would tell us stories of how Jon Alex was influencing her. I would think, *How is that possible? He can't even speak.*

Connie would insist that there was simply something about him. My wife Becky began to encourage Connie to stay for the second service at our church after helping with Jon Alex during the first service.

After a while, Connie began to hang around for the next service after the one we attended. Every week she would serve Jon Alex at the first service, and then attend the second service. Connie says it was hard at first because she was all alone and sat by herself. But each week, Connie says she began to feel stronger and stronger in the Lord. She found his grace and unconditional love. She found the God she had been looking for all her life.

At our church, if you so choose, we allow for whoever has been the biggest spiritual influence in your life to baptize you. Connie chose my son Jon Alex. She said in her baptism testimony, "Jon Alex was the perfect person God put in my life."

Together as a family, Becky, Jon Alex, and myself had the privilege of baptizing Connie. Before long, Connie didn't have to sit by herself anymore as several members of Connie's family began to attend with her. I remember looking down from stage one Sunday and seeing an entire pew filled by her family.

Connie has become a dear friend of ours. When her first husband died rather unexpectedly, I performed the celebration of his life ceremony. This summer, Connie remarried a man that she now attends church with together. I was honored and privileged to unite them in marriage. God's story continues.

I'm still in awe of what God did. Jon Alex's story became intertwined with Connie's story. And now our family's story includes Connie's story. But both of our stories are just part of God's story. They have become bits of fabric that God is using to weave his tapestry in the telling of his story.

"You intended to harm me, but God intended it all for good. He brought me to this position so I could save the lives of many people."

Let him tell his story through your life. Every life can be used by God to bring glory to his name. Your story isn't over.

Chapter 13
GOD'S MASTERPIECE

Now it's sixteen years later. God has still chosen not to heal my son. He is still autistic. He still has cerebral palsy. He still has seizures. He still requires our 24/7 care as he is developmentally disabled. In many ways, he is still like a baby. He will live in our house with us all of his life.

Our life has been so hard. The journey and path God has sent us down has been challenging, trying, and sometimes brutally difficult. But if I could go back now and have God answer my prayers differently, I would not.

God, in his sovereignty, has chosen not to heal my son. Instead, God has used my son to heal me. And now I believe God is using my son's life to help bring healing to others. He sent a broken child into a broken world to a broken father. So that together they would find God in their brokenness.

I was given the greatest blessing I could ever imagine through the gift of my son with special needs. It took me several years to figure out what God meant that night when he whispered in my spirit about the blessing he had given me. Through my son, I have experienced the presence of God in ways I could never imagine. God is using my son to reveal himself to me, to teach me, to show me things I could never have known or realized.

I was the second person to ever gaze upon my son.

The doctor let me assist in the final seconds of his birth, and I still remember watching in wonder as this 7.7 pounds, 19 inches little boy entered the world. I say I was second because while he was still in his mother's womb, his Creator knit him together. God's eyes saw his unformed body.

That same God who spoke the stars into creation, that same God who created everything out of nothing—that was the same God who wove Jon Alex together and gazed upon his form in that secret place while he created his innermost being.

And then moments before Jon Alex entered this world and my arms, God opened his book, ordained all the days of Jon Alex's life, and wrote them down before one of them came to pass.

And in that book, he wrote of a sacred purpose and a plan known only to God himself. Then he gently whispered "My son, always remember, you are fearfully and wonderfully made, for all my works are wonderful." He breathed life into my little boy, and Jon Alex opened his eyes and entered this world.

What I didn't know then, but have come to realize over the past sixteen years, is that God had given me his very self, the very essence of the gospel.

The world sees a nonverbal young man crippled by cerebral palsy, challenged cognitively, and affected by autism. The world sees a boy who cannot talk, cannot walk, and cannot function independently.

I don't see that.

I see a beautiful masterpiece.

I see a tapestry of God's grace, God's beauty, and God's love woven together on a human canvas.

The world sees paint on damp plaster. I see the ceiling of the Sistine Chapel.

The world sees a broken vessel. I see Michelangelo's *David*.

The world sees a damaged canvas. God sees a magnum opus.

If someone gives you a Picasso, you don't put it in the garage. You don't hide a work by Michelangelo in the basement. Instead, you proudly display your treasure to the world. Jon Alex is my most prized treasure.

God takes broken vessels and he uses them to make beautiful things from which he reveals himself to us. God has used my son to teach me the essence of unconditional love. God has used my son to show me how to embrace my own brokenness and accept my vulnerabilities.

I have finally understood grace and, in doing so, I have tried to become as good at giving it as I am at receiving it. I have learned that I am completely dependent upon God for all things and unable to do anything without him. And I finally realize I will not find contentment, purpose, or joy without him.

He has taught me that I don't have to understand God completely to obey God fully.

He has taught me that he really does have a plan and a purpose for everything and everyone, but I may not ever know or realize what it is.

He has used our son to teach us to revel in the simple things, find pleasure with a few things, and hope in all things.

And God has shown himself to me and demonstrated the essence of our own father and son relationship through my experiences as a dad to my own son.

Our life has been excruciatingly difficult at times. We have suffered and been though more challenges than we could have ever anticipated or imagined. We have cried oceans of tears and battled the deep waves of anguish. We have ached in our despair, and wallowed in the dark pit of hopelessness.

We have wandered among the stalagmites in the cave of autism looking for a source of light, and we have wrestled and become entangled in the snares of cerebral palsy. We have questioned God, doubted God, and pleaded with God.

And from all that, today we stand in knowledge of one simple truth.

God is good.
God is good all the time.
When we hurt ... God is good.
When we doubt ... God is good.
When we lose hope ... God is good.

When we don't understand ... God is good.
And when we cling to that which we cannot see ...
God is good.

All the time, God is good.

God makes beautiful things out of broken vessels. God creates nothing but masterpieces.

I have this beautiful son with a contagious smile and an infectious ability to bring joy and light to everyone around him. I have this living picture of how God uses the ordinary for the extraordinary. I have this breathing temple of God in my own house—the sanctuary where I see the presence of God.

I have a masterpiece.

No words may come out of my son's mouth and he can't raise his arms in praise. But make no mistake, his soul sings and dances for the Lord. Disability can affect our minds and bodies, but there are no disabled souls.

At one point on the journey, I began to feel that God gave me Jon Alex because he knew that Jon Alex needed me. I realize now that's not true. I had it all backwards.

God gave Jon Alex to me because he knew I needed Jon Alex.

Sixteen years ago, I had tried to bargain with God. I had tried to offer God a deal. I had told him that if he would only heal my son, I would testify to everyone I met just how incredible God was.

God has chosen not to heal my son this side of heaven. Instead, he has chosen to use my son to heal me.

Sixteen years ago God had said, "I've given you a blessing, what you do with it is up to you."

I have indeed been given a blessing. This book is what I chose to do with it. This has been my testimony, but this is God's story. Always remember, God's story isn't over yet, and neither is yours.

Chapter 14
MY LETTER TO JON ALEX

Dear Jon Alex,

A *letter cannot hold enough words to describe what your life has done for mine. That's why I had to write an entire book about you for the world to hear and see what God has done through your life.*

This side of heaven, you will never read my words for yourself. This world has disabled your mind and body. But this world cannot disable your soul. God has placed his spirit in you and it remains intact. I know you have a direct connection to the Spirit of God and my prayer is that he will somehow let you know what I already know.

Jon Alex, you are a world changer. You certainly changed mine. You, by your very life, are pointing people to Jesus and bringing more people into the Kingdom of God.

Before you were born, I wrote you a letter. In that letter, I gave you my definition of what success really meant. I was going to give it to you when you became a man.

In that letter, I explained what I thought was important in life and the things I felt you needed to know. I told you in that letter what living a life of success and significance meant.

I pulled that old letter out last night and read it again. I sure missed the mark in that original letter. I'm not even going to give it to you. I'm ripping it up and I'm writing this letter instead.

Turns out, my son, that you have been the teacher. I have simply been the pupil.

You saved me from myself, Jon Alex.

The impact of your life will go on for generations long after we both are in heaven playing basketball with each other.

You have become my Garden of Gethsemane, my Mount Sinai, and my burning bush where I go to meet God. Your life has been the whirlwind of the storm where God speaks to me. You have been through so much in your sixteen years of life so far. You didn't get to choose this for your life; it was given to you.

Many are the nights I begged God to give me your pain, your struggles, your special needs. Many are the nights I asked him to take everything you have that is a challenge and to give it to me instead.

God in his sovereignty chose a higher purpose for your life.

I am sure many times that I might have failed you as your dad. But know this, son: not one time have you ever failed me as a son. There is nothing you could have done, or ever could do, that will make me love you more than I already love you.

I needed the manifest presence of God in my life, so God gave me you. You didn't need healing; I was the one who needed healing.

What is success? What is it that in the end really matters and has any significance?

Success is living a life that honors God, glorifies his name, and points others to a relationship with him.

Well done, son.

Well done, his good and faithful servant.

—*Love, Dad*

EPILOGUE

Dear Autism and Cerebral Palsy,

've been meaning to write to you for quite some time, but thanks to you two, I've been quite busy as you can imagine.

Over the years, I have cursed at you, yelled at you, cried at you, and tried my best to understand you. The more I have learned about you, the more I realize how little I know about you.

But there is one thing I haven't done.

I have never stopped to thank you.

That's right. I need to stop and thank you, believe it or not.

You probably don't get a lot of thank-you notes mixed in with all your hate mail; so let me try to explain.

You see, you robbed my son of his speech. Because of you, he is nonverbal and has no language.

But when you robbed my son of his speech, God decided to give him a voice and a platform.

He may not speak, but God has used his life to inspire, bless, and teach others around him. He inspired my wife and I so much we

223

started a special-needs ministry and now we are helping encourage other families like ours on the same journey.

Hey Autism, do you remember that cave you tried to lure us and other autistic families into to live for the rest of their lives? You know, the isolated dreary cave where you want all autistic families to live in without hope?

We tried it. It just wasn't for us. So now we do search and rescue, returning to the cave over and over to show others the way out of the cave and to a better place.

Hey Cerebral Palsy, there are so many things you've robbed us from for which I need to thank you.

You've robbed me from my own pride, selfishness, and greed.
You've robbed me from my tendency to put my work above my family.
You've robbed me from living for myself instead of in service to others.
You've robbed me only caring about those who are just like me.
You've robbed me of believing there are some struggles too big for us to overcome.

I know you don't like to talk about God much since you both know what he plans to do to you someday. Ever read Revelation? But I do need to talk about him for a minute.

He made a couple of promises in a book he wrote. He promised to take what was intended to harm us and use it for good. Then he promised to make all things work together for good to accomplish his purposes.

I don't know that I ever fully believed him until we met you two and you came into our lives.

Since you two came into my life, I have met some amazing people because of our common association with you. Therapists, teachers, assistants, service providers—dedicated and passionate people who have crossed our path and have become part of our story—people I never might have met if it weren't for you. We've met so many special-needs families who are turning their trials into triumphs, too.

Speaking of books, I don't want you two to get the big head since you are featured so prominently in this book I wrote. It's not about you. It's actually God's story and how he just used you to accomplish his purposes.

God didn't take away the struggles, the pain, the challenges—he just simply used them in ways I never dreamed or you never expected.

He has used them to teach me unconditional love
He has used them to teach me the essence of grace.
He has used them to teach me to find joy in all things.
He has used them to show me how to be content in the little things.
Really, you can say he has simply used them to draw me closer to him, help me understand him, and make me stronger through him.

You really helped me take my relationship with God to a much higher and deeper level. So thank you so much! I'm so grateful! Now I rely and lean on him more than ever.

I also want to thank you for drawing my wife and me closer together in our relationship. We have learned to cry together, laugh together, grieve together, and stand strong together because of you.

So you see, Autism and Cerebral Palsy, I have quite a bit of gratitude for you. Of all the things I've said to you and about you, I've never thanked you.

Who knew that out of my seeds of hate for you could grow such love for my son and for my God?

I know you will keep trying to harm us and other families. That's just who you are and what you do.

And my God will continue to redeem all of your harm for his glory. That's just who he is and what he does.

Regards,
Jeff Davidson